Welcome

Learning to write is an important skill!
Have you ever noticed the written word is everywhere? Right now, take a moment and look around. If you are at home, you might see books, magazines, or even the daily mail set on a desk. If you are in a classroom, you might see a whiteboard with words on it, worksheets with instructions, or a note from a parent to a teacher. If you are outside, you might see signs for businesses or explaining the rules of the road. Maybe there is a newspaper stand. We communicate with each other every day with writing.

Writing also helps us to think and learn. When we write about our own ideas or what we are learning, it helps us to make connections and to reason.

Writing allows us to be creative, tell stories that make us laugh, write songs to sing, create plays for the theater, and scripts for movies.

But most of all, writing can be used to bring God glory, and it is my prayer that you learn the skill of writing to do just that. It is also my prayer this year that you learn to enjoy writing!

Yours Truly,
Fellow On-Camera Writer,
Mrs. Mora

Contents

Quick Start
02 Quick Start

FS   Flying Solo Section

LH01 **Language Helps Booklet**
LH02 Habits of Great Writers
LH03 Great Writers Follow the Writing Process
LH04 Brainstorm
LH05 Make a List
LH06 Webbing
LH07 First Rough Draft
LH08 First Input- I Can Help!
LH09 Second Rough Draft
LH10 Second Input- I Can Help/ Final Recopy
LH11 Publish and Evaluation
LH12 Quick Reference Language Charts
LH13 Capitalization Rules
LH16 End Mark Punctuation
LH17 Comma Rules
LH18 Quotation Rules
LH19 Semicolon and Colon Rules
LH20 Hyphen/Dash/Parentheses Rules
LH21 Other Editing Marks
LH22 Transitional and Linking Words
LH23 Repairing a Sentence
LH24 Words Often Confused
LH28 Writing Formats
LH29 Plural Rules More Than One
LH30 Subject Verb Agreement/Verb Tenses
LH31 Irregular Verbs Frequently Misused
LH32 Grammar Rules for Numbers
LH33 Parts of Speech
LH34 Common Literary Techniques
LH35 Sentence Types and Structure
LH36 Editing Checklist for Second Rough Draft

Worksheets for your Notebook-Paragraph Flight 2
Project #1- Oh The Places I've Been (Lessons 1-6)
Project #2- Potato People (Lessons 7-11)
Project #3- Little Help (Lessons 12-16)
Project #4- Poetry Walk/Woods (Lessons 17-21)
Project #5- Dear President (Lessons 22-26)
Project #6- Story Box Fiction (Lessons 27-32)

01

Quick Start- Setting Up Your Notebook

Benefits of Notebook Learning: Did you know that one of the best ways to learn is to keep a notebook? It's one of the best ways to learn because it puts you in charge of your learning. This book is more than just a workbook. The worksheets provided are designed to help you create a writing notebook so you can record the things you learn about writing.

1   **Gently tear out pages from this book only when you are instructed to do so.**

2   **You will need a three-ring binder with 5 dividers.**

3   **Label your dividers with the following titles:**

- **Notes** — In the notes section, insert notebook paper so you can record Knowledge Nuggets. Knowledge Nuggets are new bits of information that you discover.

- **Writing Warm-Ups** — During the year, you will be completing writing warm-ups. Writing warm-ups help you practice different writing skills. Keep all your writing warm-ups in this section.

- **Writing Projects** — In this section, you will place your project worksheets and your personal notes for your writing project.

- **Flying Solo Assignments** — **Gently tear out the pages labeled "FS" from this book and place in this section.** Check off each assignment when you complete it.

- **Language Helps Booklet** — The Language Helps Booklet is your reference guide for writing. **Gently tear out the pages labeled "LH" from this book and place in this section.**

4   **Congratulations! You are ready for your first writing lesson!**

 **Press play to learn**

Flying Solo Assignments
Flight 2: Paragraph Writing

Check off as each assignment is completed, keep for your own records.

Lesson 1	Due Date:_____	Completed

<u>Colossians 3:17 worksheet:</u>
1. Make a border around our key scripture.
2. Memorize this verse.
3. Explain what the verse means using your own words.

<u>Project: Oh, the Places I've Been</u>
1. Look at some of your family pictures from different places that you have visited.
2. On your Brainstorm Worksheet, record a place that you have visited and want to write about.

<u>Note to Parents:</u>
Students may write or dictate their writing depending on skill level.

Lesson 2	Due Date:_____	Completed

<u>Project: Oh, The Places I've Been</u>
Make a List- Make a list of how you would describe the place you have visited. Be sure to use all five of your senses.

<u>Note to Parents:</u>
Students may write or dictate their writing depending on skill level.

Lesson 3	Due Date:_____	Completed

<u>Project: Oh, The Places I've Been</u>
Complete your webbing. Do not do the shaded ovals.

<u>Note to Parents:</u>
Students may write or dictate their writing depending on skill level.

Lesson 4	Due Date:_____	Completed

<u>Project: Oh, The Places I've Been</u>
1. Complete the shaded ovals on your webbing by adding an attention-getter and closing sentence.

2. Write your First Rough Draft following the instructions in the Language Helps Booklet. Don't forget to skip lines!

<u>Note to Parents:</u>
Students may write or dictate their writing depending on skill level.

Flying Solo Assignments
Flight 2: Paragraph Writing

Check off as each assignment is completed, keep for your own records.

Lesson 5	**Due Date:**_____	**Completed**
Project: Oh, The Places I've Been 1. Read First Input sheet from class. 2. Complete your Second Rough Draft. Make changes to your project following the Second Rough Draft instructions in the Language Helps Booklet. Note to Parents: Please teach your student how to look up a word in a thesaurus. Students may write or dictate their ideas depending on their writing level.		

Lesson 6	**Due Date:**_____	**Completed**
Project: Oh, The Places I've Been 1. Final Recopy: Recopy your project into your essay folder. Follow the format in the Language Helps Booklet. 2. Complete the cover of the essay folder. Note to Parents: Students may write or dictate their ideas depending on their writing level.		

Lesson 7	**Due Date:**_____	**Completed**
Project: Oh, the Places I've Been 1. Complete Student Evaluation. 2. Next week, turn in your project with the evaluation form. 3. Publishing Assignment: Gather your family. Make them a special treat. Read your essay to them. If you have family photos from your trip, spend some time walking down memory lane! Note to Parents: Use the evaluation sheet to write encouraging notes. Students may write or dictate their ideas depending on their writing level.		
Project: Potato People Make a list describing your potato person. Remember a list does not need to be in sentence format. Note to Parents: 1. Take a picture of the newly created, "potato person" and one picture with the student and their potato person. NOTE: The photo of the potato person should be about 2" x 3" Both photos will be used in the next lesson and in lesson 11 when the student designs the essay folder cover.		

Flying Solo Assignments
Flight 2: Paragraph Writing

Check off as each assignment is completed, keep for your own records.

Lesson 8	Due Date:_____	Completed

Project: Potato People
Complete webbing. Include an attention-getter sentence and a closing sentence.

Note to Parents:
Students may write or dictate their writing depending on skill level.

Lesson 9	Due Date:_____	Completed

Project: Potato People
Write your First Rough Draft following the instructions in the Language Helps Booklet. Don't forget to skip lines!

Note to Parents:
Students may write or dictate their writing depending on skill level.

Lesson 10	Due Date:_____	Completed

Project: Potato People
1. Read Input Sheet from class.
2. Complete your Second Rough Draft.
3. Make changes to your project following the Second Rough Draft instructions in the Language Helps Booklet.

Note to Parents:
Please teach your student how to look up a word in a thesaurus. Students may write or dictate their writing depending on skill level.

Lesson 11	Due Date:_____	Completed

Project: Potato People
1. Final Recopy: Recopy your project into your essay folder. Follow the format in the Language Helps Booklet.
2. Complete the cover of the essay folder.

Note to Parents:
Students may write or dictate their writing depending on skill level.

Flying Solo Assignments
Flight 2: Paragraph Writing

Check off as each assignment is completed, keep for your own records.

Lesson 12	Due Date:_____	Completed
Project: Potato People 1. Complete Student Evaluation. Turn in your project with your evaluation form next week. 2. Publishing Assignment: Choose a friend and read your project to him or her. Show them your pictures of your potato person. Note to Parents: Use the evaluation sheet to write encouraging notes.		
Project: Little Help Make a list of the important facts about the group you have chosen. It does not need to be in sentence format. Note to Parents: Students may write or dictate their ideas depending on their writing level.		

Lesson 13	Due Date:_____	Completed
Project: Little Help Complete webbing. Add an attention-getter sentence and a closing sentence. Note to Parents: 1. Students may write or dictate their ideas depending on their writing level.		

Lesson 14	Due Date:_____	Completed
Project: Little Help Write your First Rough Draft following the instructions in the Language Helps Booklet. Don't forget to skip lines! Note to Parents: 1. Students may write or dictate their ideas depending on their writing level.		

Lesson 15	Due Date:_____	Completed
Project: Little Help 1. Read Input Sheet from class. 2. Complete your Second Rough Draft. 3. Make changes to your project following the Second Rough Draft instructions in the Language Helps Booklet. Note to Parents: Please teach your student how to look up a word in a thesaurus. Students may write or dictate their ideas depending on their writing level.		

Flying Solo Assignments
Flight 2: Paragraph Writing

Check off as each assignment is completed, keep for your own records.

Lesson 16	Due Date:_____	Completed

Project: Little Help
1. Final Re-copy: Re-copy your project into your essay folder. Follow the format in the Language Helps Booklet.
2. Complete the cover of the essay folder.
3. Publish Assignment: Send a copy of your essay to the organization that you chose. Also send copies of your project to friends and family.
4. Complete Student Evaluation.
5. Turn in your project with the Student Evaluation form next lesson.
6. Color in the Final Re-copy and Publish rectangles on your Writing Process worksheet when you are finished.

Note to Parents:
Students may write or dictate their writing depending on skill level.
Use this evaluation sheet to write encouraging notes.

Lesson 17	Due Date:_____	Completed

1. Choose a poetry book from your own collection or at the library.
2. During this unit choose a few poems to read before you write your poem.
3. ABC Poem creative worksheet-complete
4. Type poem and print following the format below;
Title of Poem
By (Your name)

REMEMBER: Use proper grammar!

Lesson 18	Due Date:_____	Completed

1. Choose a poetry book from your own collection or at the library.
2. During this unit choose a few poems to read before you write your poem.
3. Seasons Poem creative worksheet-complete.
4. Type poem and print following the format below:
Title of Poem
By (Your name)

REMEMBER: Use proper grammar!

Lesson 19	Due Date:_____	Completed

1. Choose a poetry book from your own collection or at the library.
2. During this unit choose a few poems to read before you write your poem.
3. Nursery Rhyme poem creative worksheet-complete.
4. Type poem and print following the format below:
Title of Poem
By (Your name)

REMEMBER: Use proper grammar!

Flying Solo Assignments
Flight 2: Paragraph Writing

Check off as each assignment is completed, keep for your own records.

Lesson 20 Due Date:_____	Completed
1. Choose a poetry book from your own collection or at the library. 2. During this unit choose a few poems to read before you write your poem. 3. Haiku poem creative worksheet-complete. 4. Type poem and print following the format below: Title of Poem By (Your name) REMEMBER: Use proper grammar!	

Lesson 21 Due Date:_____	Completed
1. Choose a poetry book from your own collection or at the library. 2. During this unit choose a few poems to read before you write your poem. 3. Alliteration poem creative worksheet-complete. 4. Type poem and print following the format below: Title of Poem By (Your name) Your Poem REMEMBER: Use proper grammar!	

Lesson 22 Due Date:_____	Completed

Project: Poetry Walk in the Woods
1. Complete your poetry book. It will include five poetry styles.
   • ABC Poem
   • Seasons Poem
   • Nursery Rhyme Poem
   • Haiku Poem
   • Alliteration Poem
2. Add clear contact paper to the poetry book cover to preserve this treasure!
3. Publishing Assignment: Share your poetry book with three different people.	

Project: Dear President 1. Complete the Make a List worksheet. Praise-Things you can say thank you to the president for Input-Things that you would like to see changed in America Praise-Things you like about America (It does not need to be in sentence format.) Note to Parents: Students may write or dictate their writing depending on skill.	

Flying Solo Assignments
Flight 2: Paragraph Writing

Check off as each assignment is completed, keep for your own records.

Lesson 23	Due Date:_____	Completed

Project: Dear President
1. Complete webbing. Add an attention-getter sentence and a closing sentence.

Note to Parents:
Students may write or dictate their writing depending on skill level.

Lesson 24	Due Date:_____	Completed

Project: Dear President
Write your First Rough Draft following the instructions in the Language Helps Booklet. Don't forget to skip lines! Use a respectful tone in your writing.

Note to Parents:
Students may write or dictate their writing depending on skill level.

Lesson 25	Due Date:_____	Completed

Project: Dear President
1. Read Input Sheet from class.
2. Complete your Second Rough Draft.
3. Make changes to your project following the Second Rough Draft instructions in the Language Helps Booklet.

Note to Parents:
1. Please teach your student how to look up a word in a thesaurus.
2. Students may write or dictate their writing depending on skill level.

Lesson 26	Due Date:_____	Completed

Project: Dear President
1. Recopy your project into your essay folder.
Follow business letter format given in lesson 24.
2. Complete cover of essay folder.

Note to Parents:
Students may write or dictate their writing depending on skill level.

Flying Solo Assignments
Flight 2: Paragraph Writing

Check off as each assignment is completed, keep for your own records.

Lesson 27	Due Date:_____	Completed

Project: Dear President
1. Complete Student Evaluation worksheet.
2. Turn in your project with the evaluation form next week.
3. Publish Assignment: Address envelope to the president. Refer to How to Address an Envelope below. Send your letter to the president. Don't forget the stamp!
The President
1600 Pennsylvania Ave.
Washington, D.C. 20500
*Keep a copy of your letter for your yearly portfolio.

Project: Story Box Fiction
1. Make a list of the parts of your story.
(It does not need to be in sentence format.)
2. Bring one large shoebox to your next group time.

Note to Parents:
Use evaluation sheet to write encouraging notes.
Students may write or dictate their writing depending on skill level.

How To Address An Envelope

```
My Address
1234 Main St.
Anytown, USA 54917



                    The President
                    1600 Pennsylvania Ave.
                    Washington, D.C. 20500
```

Lesson 28	Due Date:_____	Completed

Project: Story Box Fiction
1. Complete Webbing at home.
2. Add an attention-getter sentence and a closing sentence.

Note to Parents:
Students may write or dictate their writing depending on skill level.

Flying Solo Assignments
Flight 2: Paragraph Writing

Check off as each assignment is completed, keep for your own records.

Lesson 29	Due Date: _____	Completed

Project: Story Box Fiction
Write your First Rough Draft, following the instructions in the Language Helps Booklet. Don't forget to skip lines!

Note to Parents:
Students may write or dictate their writing depending on skill level.

Lesson 30	Due Date: _____	Completed

Project: Story Box Fiction
1. Read Input Sheet from class.
2. Complete your Second Rough Draft.
3. Make changes to your project following the Second Rough Draft instructions in the Language Helps Booklet.

Note to Parents:
Please teach your student how to look up a word in a thesaurus.
Students may write or dictate their writing depending on skill level.

Lesson 31	Due Date: _____	Completed

Project: Story Box Fiction
1. Final Recopy: Recopy your project into your essay folder. Follow the format in the Here to Help Learning Language Helps Booklet.
2. Complete the cover of the essay folder.
3. Bring in your Yearly Writing Portfolio (See "Make a Yearly Writing Portfolio" in the Writing Overview.) Make sure all your completed writing projects are placed in the folder. You will have the opportunity to share your favorite project with your group.

Flight 2 Launching Paragraph Writing
Oh, the Places I've Been
Potato People
Little Help
Poetry Pop-up Book
Dear President
Story Box Fiction

Note to Parents:
Students may write or dictate their writing depending on skill level.

Flying Solo Assignments
Flight 2: Paragraph Writing

Check off as each assignment is completed, keep for your own records.

Lesson 32	Due Date:_____	Completed
Project: Story Box Fiction 1. Complete Student Evaluation. 2. Publish Assignment: Find a community display opportunity such as a library, county fair or end of year co-op party to display story box and story. 3. See you on the next flight! A special note from Knucklehead: Please send a self-addressed stamped envelope with a note to addressed to Knucklehead. Tell him which writing project was your favorite and why. He will send you his personal "Pencils Up" stickers! Knucklehead's address can be found at HereToHelpLearning.com. Note to Parents: Use this evaluation sheet to write encouraging notes. Students may write or dictate their writing depending on skill level.		

Habits of Great Writers

Great writers will...
- Read a lot of great books!
- Observe the world around them.
- Keep a writing notebook to jot down ideas.
- Make writing goals.
- Never stop learning about how to write more effectively.
- Ask others for feedback.
- Take input and criticism well.
- Use their imagination.
- Remove all distractions when they write.
- Write often.

Did you know...
Many great writers, when they were young, dictated their stories to a parent?

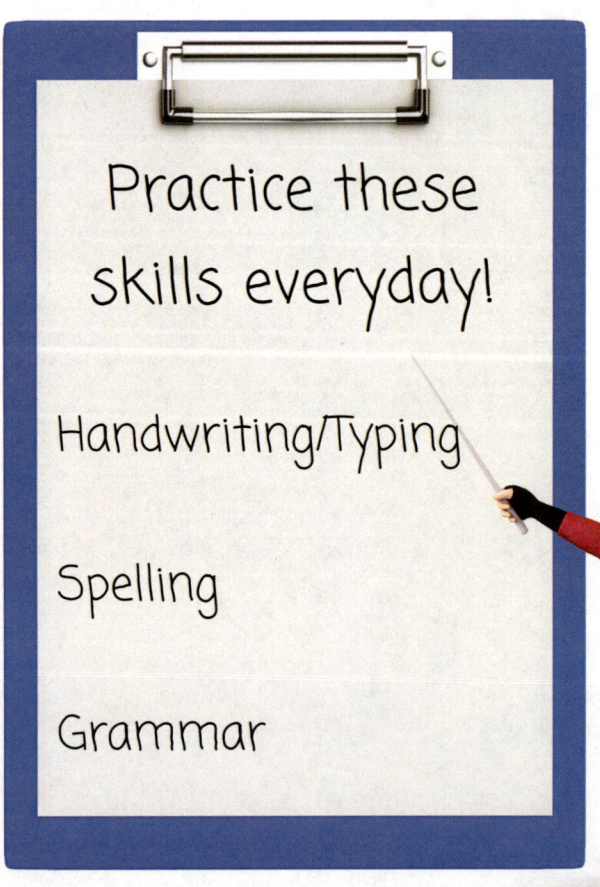

Practice these skills everyday!

Handwriting/Typing

Spelling

Grammar

Great Writers Follow the Writing Process

The **Writing Process** is a series of steps a writer completes to produce a finished writing project.

The **Writing Process** helps a writer stay focused.

The **Writing Process** helps prevent writer's block.

The **Writing Process** can be used by everyone, even a beginner!

Each time you travel the writing process you will become a better writer!

Each step of the Writing Process explained...

Step 1 - Brainstorm

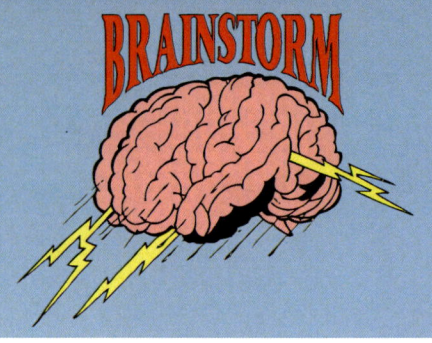

Skill to Learn: Learn to generate ideas for writing.

Hand Motion/Memory Aid: Teacher and Student Say- "Brainstorm!"
(Put both hands on head with fingers spread out and massage your head.)

Explanation

Learning to generate writing ideas requires learning how to remove barriers to creativity. It helps to understand the roles of the right and left side of the brain. The right side of our brain loves to create. The left side of our brain loves to organize things into lists and make decisions. However, it is very difficult for the right side of our brain to create while the left side of the brain is organizing and deciding what will make a good writing project and what will not.

How do we make the right side of our brain happy while it is thinking of writing ideas? It's easy when you follow the rules for brainstorming.

Use a Timer

1. First, we need to prevent the left side of the brain from making lists by using a blank piece of paper with no lines. Write all over the paper: sideways, diagonal, start at the bottom.

2. Next, set a timer for 2-3 minutes. The right side of our brain loves the excitement of fast paced thinking.

3. The ultimate secret of unlocking our creative right side of our brain is NO judgments. That means do not stop and judge an idea. Don't say, "I don't want to write about that subject." The trick is to come up with as many ideas as possible. **The win in brainstorming is how many ideas are generated.**

No Judgements

4. Now it's time to engage the left side of our brain and make decisions. Circle your top three ideas.

5. Okay, now that you have done that, sit back, look, and consider which of the three topics you would like to write about.

6. Choose one writing topic. Put a star by your choice.

7. If you think of a better idea at a later time, you are free to use it. Sometimes just participating in the brainstorming step will unlock further ideas.

Step 2-Make a List

Skill to Learn: Learn to gather information.

Hand Motion Memory Aid: Teacher and Student Say-"Make a List!"
(Put left hand out, with palm up. With right hand, pretend to write on the open hand. The last flourish of pretend writing flies into the air.)

Explanation:
The road to organized writing begins with gathering information. Gathering information on a subject helps to clarify direction. Worksheets are provided to assist you. Your list needs only to contain words or word phrases. It does not need to be in sentence format.

> The next best thing to knowing something is knowing where to find it.
> Samuel Johnson

Sources of information:

Bible
-Word search
-Topical study

Personal Experiences
-Memories
-Observation
-Imagination
-Talk with family members
-Family photo albums

Outside Sources
-Books
-Magazines
-Library
-Internet
-DVDs or Video
-Interviews
-Local news source

Step 3-Webbing

Skill to Learn: Learn to organize information.

Hand Motion Memory Aid: Teacher and Student Say-Webbing!
(Both hands are held up with palm facing out. Spread fingers out and wiggle them.)

Explanation:

In the Webbing step, you will evaluate your list and begin to organize your information, grouping like ideas together and eliminating ideas that don't support the topic. Worksheets are provided to help you organize your information and ideas.

1. Read the headings in each webbing oval on your worksheet.
2. Evaluate your list items and place it in the correct oval on your webbing.

Questions to Ask Yourself
- Which ideas are more similar?
- When did it happen, in the beginning, middle, or the end of your story?
- Which idea or piece of information does not belong in the story?
- What part of your story is missing? What do you need to add?

3. Add Attention-Getter and Closing Sentences

Attention-Getter Sentence: This is the main idea or topic sentence of the paragraph. Your goal is to write in such a way that grabs the attention of your reader.

Closing Sentence: This is the concluding sentence. It finishes your writing or story. It helps to sum up your ideas and if written well, will make your reader say, "Well done!"

Helpful Hints:
- Talk about your ideas.
- Write two Attention-Getter and Closing sentences and then ask others for input. The question to ask is, does this sentence grab your attention? Do you want to continue reading my story?
- Choose a different type of sentence structure. (See Sentence Types and Structure in the Language Helps Booklet.)
- Look for examples of good Attention-Getter and Closing Sentences in the stories you read and record them in your notebook.

Step 4-First Rough Draft

Skill to Learn: Learn to express your thoughts and ideas through writing.

Hand Motion Memory Aid: Teacher and Student Say- First Rough Draft! (Scoop your body down low, say the word "rough" like a dog barking, and finish with your head all the way back.)

Explanation:
During group time, prepare to write your First Rough Draft by talking about your ideas. Discussing your ideas is important before you begin to write.
During the Flying Solo or independent time, write or dictate your story.

1. Learn and review "colorful words" (strong descriptive words):
- **Ask questions that help the reader "see" the story better.**

What specific noun can you use? Do some research. Example: What kind of horse? An Arabian horse.
How would you describe _____? How would you make a sentence?
Tell me more about_____ in the story? How would you make a sentence?

- **Ask questions that help the reader "hear" the story better.**

How would you describe the sound?
How did the character say_____?
What kind of voice does your character have?
What did it sound like? Look up a word that would describe what you just said.

- **Ask questions that help the reader "taste" the story better.**

Where in your story can you include a description of how something tasted?
Can you compare a taste to something else?

- **Ask questions that help the reader "smell" the story better.**

Where in your story can you include a description of how something smelled?
Can you compare the smell to something else?

- **Ask questions that help the reader "feel" the story better.**

If I touched the object, what would it feel like? (physical)
Can you compare how it feels to something else?
What was the character feeling at that moment? (emotional)

2. Learn and review Transitional Words: Choose a transitional word from the list in the Language Helps Booklet and use it in a sentence for your project.

Meet Beth the Bolter, your writing mechanic. She helps your students prepare to write the First Rough Draft.

Remember: The First Rough Draft is your first attempt at getting your ideas on paper. It does not have to be perfect. Give yourself a large block of uninterrupted time. Begin by reviewing your list and webbing. Think about the ideas you talked about in your group time and begin with writing or dictating your attention-getter sentence. Keep moving forward in your story. You will have an opportunity to fix it later in the writing process.

Step 5-First Input "I Can Help!" (Content)

Skill to Learn: Learn to give and receive input from others. The focus in this step is on the content of the story and not grammar or spelling.

Hand Motions/Memory Aid: Teacher and Student Say–"First Input! I Can Help!" (Raise and shake hand trying to touch ceiling)

Explanation: Have you ever looked at the front pages of a book? Most books have an acknowledgement page or thank you page. If you read these pages, you will usually find a place where the author showers a list of people with praise and gratitude for the help they gave to the author during the writing of their book. All successful writers get help and input on their writing. In the First Input, you will learn to receive and give input on the **content of your writing**.

Be a Great PIPer!
PIP stands for Praise-Input-Praise
1. Practice the Rules of Respect.

Be a Great Presenter!
1. Practice the Rules of Respect.

Rules of Respect
1. Make eye contact.
2. Smile, smile, smile!
3. Lots of pleases and thank yous!
4. Think, think, think! Ask great questions!
5. Find knowledge nuggets!

2. **PRAISE:** Offer to the presenter what you liked about the story. Be specific.
Example: I loved the description of the rainbow.
3. **INPUT:** Offer input by asking questions about the story. Be specific. Example: Where was the boy standing when he saw the rainbow?

2. Read with a loud clear voice.
3. Listen carefully to all the input.
4. Say thank you when you receive input.
5. You don't have to use every input, but you do need to be grateful.

Help the presenter by identifying "Dead Words". Dead words are overused words.

4. **PRAISE:** Offer to the presenter encouraging words. Example: I really enjoyed the ending of your story. I can't wait to see the details you are going to add!

I didn't know that! Hey! I found a Knowledge Nugget! I like Knowledge Nuggets!

Step 6-Second Rough Draft

Skill to Learn: Learn to revise content after receiving input.

Motion Memory Aid: Teacher and Student Say- Second Rough Draft! (Scoop your body down low, say the word "rough" like a dog barking, and finish with your head all the way back.)

Explanation: No one writes perfectly the first time, and every writing project can be improved. The Second Rough Draft step gives you the opportunity to take a second look at your writing.

1. Read input worksheet/s from last step.
2. Read your project out loud.
3. Identify areas that need to be changed.
4. Use the Editing Checklist for the Second Rough Draft. (See your Language Helps Booklet)
5. Write small changes in-between lines.
6. Use editing marks found in the Language Helps Booklet.
7. Change "dead words" by looking up stronger words in a thesaurus.
8. Follow the example below to to add larger amounts to your writing.

O.C.H.A. or Organizational Composition Home Authority reminds you what to do and look for in the Second Rough Draft.

Maybe you will win the **O.C.H.A.** Second Rough Draft Safety Award!

How to Add to Your First Rough Draft

LH 09

Step 7-Second Input "I Can Help!" (Grammar and Spelling)

Skill to Learn: Learn to discover grammar and spelling errors in your writing.

Hand Motions/Memory Aid: Teacher and Student Say-Second Input "I Can Help!" (Raise and shake hand trying to touch ceiling)

Explanation: Your teacher becomes your editor, and together you will make final corrections on content, grammar, and spelling.

Helpful Hints:
- Learn something new about grammar or spelling.
- Learn editing marks. (See Language Helps Booklet)
- Record what you learn in the note section of your notebook.

Step 8-Final Recopy

Skill to Learn: Learn to present your work with excellence.

Hand Motions/Memory Aid: Teacher and Student Say: Final Recopy! (The word is said with your tongue sticking out and off to the side as you pretend to recopy a paper. Why the tongue sticking out? Because when I was a child, my mother said I could not concentrate unless my tongue was sticking out.)

Explanation: In this step, you will prepare your writing for the last step in the writing process, which is publish.

1. Recopy your project into an essay folder following the format in the Language Helps Booklet unless instructed differently. Neatness counts.
2. Create a cover. Cover templates and examples are provided for all projects.
3. Read your project out loud to catch any recopying errors.

Step 9-Publish

Skill to Learn: Learn to share your writing.

Hand Motions/Memory Aid: Teacher and Student Say-Publish and publish means to share. (Both hands are together with palms facing up and then are moved forward.)

Explanation: The writing process finishes with sharing or publishing your writing project. Sharing your project will help you become a better writer. Each writing project has a unique publishing assignment. You will have the opportunity to share your writing with people you know such as your grandma, grandpa, aunts, uncles, teachers, church leaders, homeschool contacts, and community leaders.

Make a yearly portfolio to keep your finished writing projects.

1. Gather Supplies
- 28" x 22" poster board- any color
- Standard stapler
- Glue stick
- Marker
- Front cover (Lesson 1)

2. Fold poster board lengthwise from the bottom, approximately 6 inches.

3. Fold poster board in half widthwise.

4. Using a standard stapler, staple the side of the folded poster board to create a pocket. (Make sure the staple folds point inside the created folder.) Glue the cover to the front and decorate.

Evaluation

Explanation: Writers never stop learning and growing! Before you begin the next project, it is important to identify the parts of your project that you did well and the parts of your project you can improve. Each writing project has a simple self-evaluation form. Complete the form and share it with your teacher. Talk with your teacher about your next writing goals. You are on the road to becoming a better writer!

LH
11

Quick Reference Language Charts

Could you imagine what would happen if there were no rules for driving a car on the road? Many people would get hurt, and it would also take twice as long to get anywhere. Rules are important. The rules of language are important too! Using proper spelling, punctuation, and grammar help your reader understand what you write.

On the following pages, there are 24 Quick Reference Language Charts. Right now, you might be thinking, "Wow, that's a lot of rules!" I will admit, there are a lot of rules. However, the good news is you can learn them a little at a time. I hope you are practicing your spelling and grammar every day. It will help you become a better writer.

You will be glad to know that even professional writers search for answers to their grammar, punctuation, or spelling questions in reference guides and get help from their editors. Remember, when in doubt, look it up and don't hesitate to ask your parent or teacher for help.

Capitalization

Editing Mark	Use of Editing Mark	Example
≡	Change to a capital letter	antonio climbed a tree.
/	Change to a lower case letter	Antonio climbed a Tree.

Rule Number	Rule	Example
1	The first word of every sentence	Sarah is a wonderful writer.
2	The word "I"	My rabbit and I won first place.
3	Days of the week	Monday, Tuesday, Wednesday, Thursday, Friday, Saturday, Sunday
4	Months of the year	January, February, March, April, May, June, July, August, September, October, November, December
5	Holidays	Christmas, Thanksgiving, Easter
6	The salutation or greeting of a letter	Dear Grandma,
7	The closing of a letter	Love, Yours Truly, Sincerely, From
8	People's first and last names	John Sonoma Martha Washington
9	Titles or their abbreviations when used with a name	Captain John Smith-Capt. Doctor Jane Lewis-Dr. President-Pres. Mister-Mr. or Mistress- Mrs. Lieutenant-Lt. Queen Elizabeth
10	Towns	Portland, Detroit, Rio de Janiero
11	Counties	Los Angeles County, El Dorado County
12	States	New York, Pennsylvania
13	Countries	Canada, England, France, Turkey
14	Continents	Africa, Asia, Europe, North America, South America, Antarctica, Australia
15	Islands	Long Island, West Indies, Florida Keys, Liberty Island
16	Mountains	Swiss Alps, Appalachian Mountains, Mount of Olives
17	Bodies of water	Pacific Ocean, Mississippi River, Lake Michigan
18	Parks	Grand Canyon National Park Lotus County Park

Capitalization

Rule Number	Rule	Example
19	Planets Stars Constellations	Mars Polaris Little Dipper
20	Regions North, South, East, and West only when they refer to a place, NOT direction	The North, New England, the Middle West *Be careful! If you are speaking of a direction, you do NOT capitalize north, south, east, or west. Correct: I will travel to the Northwest with my family. Incorrect: We will travel North five miles before turning right.
21	Roads Streets Highways	Green Valley Road Farmers Avenue Sunrise Highway
22	Nationalities and languages	French, Russian, Mexican, Asian
23	Ships Planes Spacecrafts	*Mayflower* *Air Force One* *Columbia* Note: These proper nouns need to be italicized or underlined.
24	Buildings Monuments	White House Statue of Liberty
25	Organizations	Boy Scouts of America National Basketball Association
26	Teams	Dallas Cowboys River Cats
27	Historic Events	Civil War Gold Rush
28	Special Events	Nebraska Home School Convention Florida Special Olympics
29	Awards	Purple Heart Key Club Community Award
30	Businesses	Here To Help Learning Chick-Fil-A
31	Government Agencies	Federal Bureau of Investigation House of Representatives
32	Schools and Institutions	Rancho Mora School United States Air Force
33	Books Magazines Newspapers Movies TV programs	*Winnie the Pooh* *Highlights* (magazine) *New York Times* (newspaper) *It's a Wonderful Life* *Sesame Street* Note: These titles need to be italicized or underlined.
34	Poems Short stories Music Name of chapter in a book	"The Swing" "The Make-Over Club" "Amazing Grace" "Mom's Day Out"-name of a chapter Note: Poems, stories, name of chapter, and songs are placed in quotations.
35	Historical Documents	Declaration of Independence U.S. Constitution Magna Carta

Capitalization

Rule Number	Rule	Example
36	Works of art	*La Pietá* *The Thinker* ***Note: These titles need to be italicized or underlined.***
37	Religions and their followers	**C**hristian- **C**hristians **J**udaism- **J**ewish
38	Holy Writings	**B**ible, **D**ead **S**ea **S**crolls
39	Referring to the Creator of universe	**G**od
40	First letter in a quotation	He said, "**I**t's time to go!" She said, "**W**ait, I will come!" Be careful; the first letter is not capitalized if the speaker continues to speak after a descriptive phrase. <u>Correct</u>: "When I get home," John interrupted Sean, "you will get your present." <u>Incorrect</u>: "When I get home," John interrupted Sean, "You will get your present."
41	Proper Adjectives	**M**artian landscape **T**urkish border
42	A word that is used as a name	I had so much fun with **M**om and **A**unt **S**ue. *Be careful; don't use a capital when it is not used as someone's name. <u>**Check yourself**</u>: -If you can replace the word with a name, and it sounds correct, then it needs a capital letter. **Example:** I had so much fun with <u>M</u>om and <u>A</u>unt <u>S</u>ue. *Check: I had so much fun with Linda and Aunt Sue. This makes sense. This sentence is correct! **Example:** I had so much fun with my <u>M</u>om and my <u>A</u>unt. *Check: I had so much fun with my <u>Linda</u> and my <u>Sue</u>. This does not make sense. This sentence is <u>NOT</u> correct. Correct: I had so much fun with my mom and my aunt.

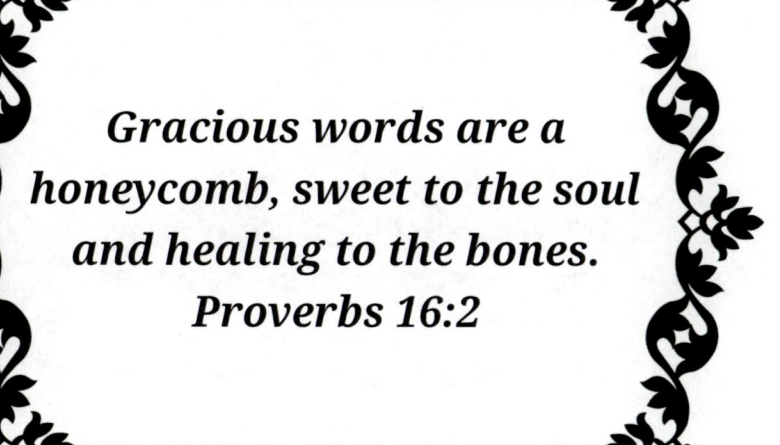

Gracious words are a honeycomb, sweet to the soul and healing to the bones.
Proverbs 16:2

End Mark Rules

Editing Mark	Use of Editing Mark	Example
⊙	Add a period	Megan brought her homework⊙
℘	Remove a period	Megan brought.her homework.
?∧	Add a question mark	Who is coming to breakfast ?∧
℘	Remove a question mark	Who? is coming to breakfast?
!∧	Add an exclamation point	Look out∧
℘	Remove an exclamation point	She set the dishes on the table!

Rule #	Rule	Example
1	Use a period for statement sentences.	Helen is a talented artist.
2	Use a question mark to ask a question	Are your teeth brushed?
3	Use an exclamation point to show excitement	I can't believe we are going to the beach tomorrow! Ouch!
4	Use a period for abbreviations	Mr. Mrs. Dr. a.m. p.m. lb. oz. in. gal.

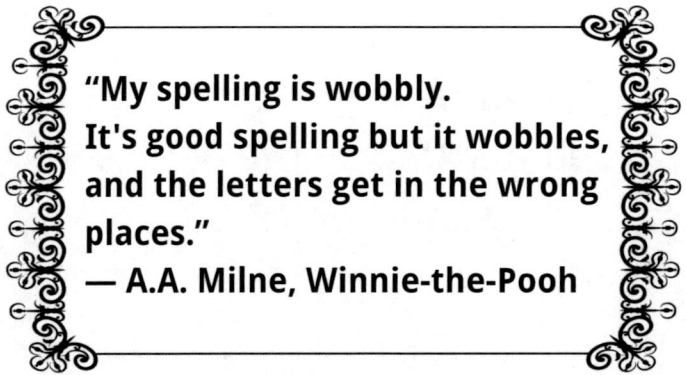

"My spelling is wobbly.
It's good spelling but it wobbles,
and the letters get in the wrong places."
— A.A. Milne, Winnie-the-Pooh

Comma Rules

Editing Mark	Use of Editing Mark	Example
⌃ (comma insert)	Add a comma	Caitlyn, Grace, and Tiffany smiled for the camera.
⌒ (loop)	Remove a comma	Yours, Truly,

Rule Number	Rule	Example
1	Words in a series or list	Please take the balls, gloves, and bases down to the field.
2	After an interjection (A word that shows emotion and can stand alone) or after an introductory phrase	**Wow**, I thought Walker did a fabulous job! **Well**, I'll think about it. "**Yes**, we would love to go on the field trip."
3	After or before someone's name that is set apart from the sentence	**Hannah**, please take care of your sister. Please take care of your sister, **Hannah**. Please, **Hannah**, take care of your sister.
4	After someone speaks in a direct quotation	Chayden asked, "Do you want to jump on the trampoline?" "Yes I would," replied Walter.
5	Before or after a short clause	Skipping through the meadow, Sally sang loudly. In my opinion, you should try out for the team.
6	Before or after a word that interrupts the main sentence	The art supplies, however, melted in the hot sun.
7	Before or after a phrase that describes a noun	Ken Burkey, our pastor, prayed for everyone. Our pastor, Ken Burkey, prayed for everyone. Mrs. Conca, our friend, served in a Mexican orphanage.
8	Connecting two sentences into a compound sentence with a conjunction such as, *and, but, or, for, nor, or, so, yet*	Annemarie ate her banana, but Antonio chose to play.
9	Two adjectives that describe the same noun	**A comma is needed**-The giraffe is a tall, graceful animal. **No comma is needed**-The giraffe has dark yellow hair. Be careful: <u>Check #1</u>-To check if a comma is needed, switch the order of the adjectives. Does it make sense? If yes, then it needs a comma. If no, then it does not need a comma. **Yes**-comma-The giraffe is a graceful, tall animal. **No**-comma-The giraffe has yellow dark hair. <u>Check #2</u>-To check if a comma is needed, put the word "and" in between the adjectives. If it makes sense, use a comma. **Yes**-comma-The giraffe is a tall (and) graceful animal. **No**-comma-The giraffe has dark (and) yellow hair.
10	After a name followed by an abbreviation	My brother, Gerald Edward Kopsisckis Jr., constructs laboratories for chemical engineers.

Quotation Rules

Editing Mark	Use of Editing Mark	Example
⋁"	Add quotation marks	Asher said, ⋁"Can you play with me?"
◯	Remove quotation marks	Zack "answered, "Of course I will."

Rule Number	Rule	Example
1	Quotation marks go around the words that someone has directly spoken	Mattea said, "I love school! Don't you?"
2	Commas and question marks go inside the quotation marks	"I sure do," said Sophia. "Are you coming to the party?" John asked.
3	Indent every time a new person speaks.	→"Me too," said Emma. →"I can't wait to see what experiments we do in science today!" said Lily. →"Maybe it will be something messy," said Mia.
4	Capitalize the first word in a direct quote	Mother said, "**S**pring is my favorite time of year."
5	Capitalize the first word in an interrupted quote but not the first word of the second part of the sentence.	"**Y**our books," whispered Mom, "**a**re on the front porch." Note: The first part of the quote is capitalized. Note: The second part of the quote is the completion of the sentence. Therefore, the first word of the second quote is not capitalized. Hint: Read both parts of the sentence together and ask yourself if it is a complete sentence. Example: "Your books are on the front porch," whispered Mom.

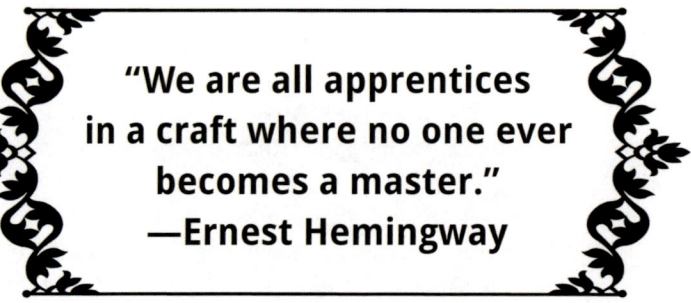

"We are all apprentices in a craft where no one ever becomes a master."
—Ernest Hemingway

Semicolon Rules

Editing Mark	Use of Editing Mark	Example
⁀;⁀	Add a semicolon	Bethany stood at the library door; she blinked in disbelief.
⌀	Remove a semicolon	Garret saw what; was coming.

Rule Number	Rule	Example
1	Use like a comma joining two independent or complete sentences	Abby-Rain also saw the new shipment of library books arrive; her eyes popped.
2	You may use a semicolon instead of a comma	Hannah jumped for joy; in the meantime, her mother smiled with pride at her love of reading. Be careful: You may not use a semicolon when the sentences are joined by the conjunctions and, but, or, nor, so, or yet.

Colon Rules

Editing Mark	Use of Editing Mark	Example
⁀:⁀	Add a colon	It is 3:00 a.m.
⌀	Remove a colon	Can you bring: towels, suntan lotion, and a snack?

Rule #	Rule	Example
1	To mean "note what follows"	Please bring to summer camp: towels, a sweatshirt, a Bible, extra socks, and suntan lotion. Be careful: Do not use a colon before a list that follows a verb. Incorrect: Can you bring: towels, suntan lotion and a snack?
2	Before a long statement or quotation	George Washington said: "The foolish and the wicked practice of profane cursing and swearing is a vice so mean and low that every person of sense and character detests and despises it."
3	Time	8:30 a.m.
4	Greeting in a business letter	Dear Mr. President:
5	Between Bible verses	John 3:16

LH 19

Hyphen/Dash/Parentheses Rules

Editing Mark	Use of Editing Mark	Example
∧	Add a hyphen	The semi sweet chocolate chips were delicious. ∧
ᓚ	Remove a hyphen	I want to know more-about frogs.

Rule #	Rule	Example
1	Between numbers	One-half Three-quarters Half-ton
2	Two words that join together to make an adjective that describes a noun	Semi-sweet chocolate Hard-boiled eggs Full-time student
3	To divide a word at the end of a line	• There should be at least two letters plus the hyphen on the first line and at least three letters on the second line. Do not divide between pages. Hyphen is placed on the first line. • To divide syllables "bat-tle. • Do not divide proper nouns or adjectives, such as "Washington" or "Chinese".
4	Use a dash to set apart a break in conversation or thought	"How many times have I asked you—" she stopped talking and starred out the window.
5	Use parentheses to insert an explanation into a complete sentence	The wedding dress (twenty-five years old) hung in the closet.

"No tears in the writer,
no tears in the reader.
No surprise in the writer,
no surprise in the reader."
— Robert Frost

Other Editing Marks

Editing Mark	Use of Editing Mark	Example
(SP)	Spelled incorrectly	We ran into the (feild). [SP above]
∨'	Add apostrophe	I dont know what to do. [∨' above]
‿	Join words together or close a gap	To‿day, we will celebrate!
(SP)	Spell out the word	My sister is 2 years old. [(SP) above]
∂	Delete	I can't tell you how much ~~a very very very much~~ I want to go to the game.
¶	Start a new paragraph and indent	"Is that your sister?" I asked. ¶ "Yes, it is!" Garret answered.
Frag.___	Fragment: incomplete sentence	Frag. Ran through the meadow with his tail wagging.
R.O.___	Run-on: two or more sentences incorrectly joined	R.O. Justin loved to travel in outer space he felt it was his best adventure to date.

LH
21

Transitional and Linking Words

Add Information	Summary	Compare	Make a point
Again	In short	But	Again
Besides	Finally	Otherwise	Indeed
Moreover	In summary	Even though	To repeat
Another	In conclusion	Conversely	Truly
For instance	Consequently	Even so	In fact
Together with	Due to	Yet	To emphasize
And	As a result	However	For this reason
Likewise	Accordingly	Counter to	With this in mind
As well	To sum up	On the other hand	
Furthermore	Thus	As opposed to	
Additionally	Therefore		
Along with			
Also			
For example			
Equally important			
Further			

Same	Make clear	Where	Time
In the same manner	In other words	Above	About
In the same way	Put another way	Across	After
Also	Stated differently	Against	At
Likewise	To clarify	Along	First
Like	For instance	Alongside	Second
Both		Amid	Third
As		In front of	Prior to
Similarly		Near	Subsequently
		Among	Until
		Around	Meanwhile
		Away from	Today
		In back of	Tomorrow
		Behind	Before
		Below	Soon
		Inside	Afterward
		Beneath	Immediately
		Beside	Finally
		Between	During
		Beyond	Next
		Down	As soon as
		Into	Then
		Onto	
		On top of	
		Throughout	
		Outside	
		To the right	
		Over	
		Under	

Repairing a Sentence

A fragment is an incomplete sentence.

All sentences must have a subject and a verb. A fragment is an incomplete sentence. Either the subject, the verb, or both are missing. To fix a fragment, find out what is missing and add the missing parts.
Example:
Correct: The puppy ran through the meadow with his tail wagging.
Missing subject: Ran through the meadow with his tail wagging.
Missing verb: The puppy with his tail wagging.
Missing both subject and verb: With his tail wagging.
The editing mark is "Frag." and the fragment is underlined.

Frag. Ran through the meadow with his tail wagging.

A run-on sentence is when two or more complete sentences are joined incorrectly. There are four easy ways to fix them.

  1. **Add a period.**

Incorrect: Justin loved to travel in outer space he felt it was his best adventure to date.
Correct: Justin loved to travel in outer space. He felt it was his best adventure to date.

  2. **Add a semicolon.**

Incorrect: Justin loved to travel in outer space he felt it was his best adventure to date.
Correct: Justin loved to travel in outer space; he felt it was his best adventure to date.

  3. **Add a conjunction or connecting word.**

*Famous connecting words: and, but, or, yet
*Be careful: Use a comma after the first independent sentence and before the connecting word.
Incorrect: Justin loved to travel in outer space he felt it was his best adventure to date.
Correct: Justin loved to travel in outer space, and he felt it was his best adventure to date.

  4. **Add a transitional word.**

*Use your transitional word list.
*Be careful, you must use a semi-colon before the transitional word and a comma after it to offset the transitional word.

Incorrect: Justin loved to travel in outer space he felt it was his best adventure to date.
Correct: Justin loved to travel in outer space; however, he felt it was his best adventure to date.

The editing mark is "R.O." and the run-on sentence is underlined.

R.O. Justin loved to travel in outer space he felt it was his best adventure to date.

Misplaced or Dangling Modifiers
A dangling modifier is a word or word phrase that is confusing . To fix a dangling or misplaced modifier keep the descriptive words close to what is being described. You may need to add a noun or verb to make a clear sentence.

Misplaced modifier: I read about the bank robbers who were captured in the evening paper.
(It sounds like the robbers were apprehended in the newspaper.)
Correct: I read this morning's paper about the bank robbers who were captured.

Dangling Modifier: Equipped with even the best climbing tools, the steep canyon was difficult to climb.
(It sounds like the canyon was the subject that was equipped and doing the climbing.)
Correct: Equipped with even the best climbing tools, the mountaineers had difficulty climbing the steep canyon.

LH

Words Often Confused

accept-to receive or take except-not including	I **accept** your encouragement. The market is open everyday **except** Sunday.
affect-(verb) to influence effect-(noun) as a result	Your input will **affect** my decision. The **effect** of hard work results in success.
"alot" is not a word. a lot-a large amount allot-(verb)	We can learn **a lot** from studying. Please **allot** ample time to write.
advice- (noun) counsel advise-(verb) to give advice	My **advice** is take time to be grateful. I would **advise** you to research your subject.
all ready-(pronoun and adjective) everyone is ready already-(adverb) by a certain time	We are **all ready** for our vacation. We are **already** finished.
all together-everyone in the same place altogether-entirely	When we were **all together**, we sat down and ate dinner. It was **altogether** the wrong color.
brake-a stopping device. break- to shatter	Use the **brake** to stop the car. If you drop the glass it might **break**.
bring-use in relation to an end point or destination. take-use in relationship to a starting point	**Bring** your schoolwork to me. Please **take** the dog for a walk.
capital-upper case letter capital-money capital-punishable by death capital -excellent capital-center of government capitol- Building or statehouse	Use a **capital** letter at the beginning of a sentence. We need **capital** to start our business. **Capital** punishment is reserved for severe crimes. What a **capital** idea for the fundraiser. Sacramento is the **capital** of California. In Sacramento, the **capitol** is located on 10th Street.
choose-(verb-present and future tense) chose-(verb-past tense) (Rhymes with goes)	I **choose** the red crayon. You may **choose** any color crayon. The boys **chose** to play outside.
coarse- crude or rough course-path of action course-unit of study course -part of a meal course-naturally or certainly	She never uses **coarse** language. The fabric was too **coarse** for a dress. The frazzled duck flew off its **course**. My literature class was an excellent **course**. The appetizer **course** was my favorite. Of **course** you are invited!

Words Often Confused

Complement-to complete Compliment-praise or accolade	The lamp I chose **complemented** the living room. She was grateful for the **compliment** on her work.
could have=could've would have=would've should have=should've	Do not write "could of" Do not write "would of" Do not write "should of"
desert-(noun) dry region desert-(verb) to leave dessert-(noun) final course of a meal	The **desert** is home to many animals. Do not **desert** your post. The **dessert** was cherry pie.
fewer-how many. Use with nouns that you can count such as dogs, houses, and pens less-how much. Use with singular nouns such as money, time, and traffic.	There are **fewer** blossoming trees this year. There is **less** time spent complaining.
for-belong to Four-the number four	This present is **for** you! The number **four** is an even number.
formally-proper formerly-in the past	How would you like to be **formally** introduced? The new employee was **formerly** a government representative.
good-(adjective) high quality good-(adjective) describes how something or someone "is" happy or pleased well-(adverb)-skillful, positive well-(adjective)-good health or satisfactory.	We read a **good** book. I feel **good** today. He played the violin **well**. He is **well** today.
hear-to receive sounds here-place	I can **hear** you speak. Please meet me **here** next week.
its-possessive of "it" it's-(contraction) means "it is"	The dog stopped **its** barking. **It's** a beautiful day.
lead-(verb, present tense) to go first led-(verb, past tense) to go first lead-a heavy metal	She will **lead** the way. Last month, she **led** us to victory! **Lead** is sometimes used to make fishing weights.

LH

Words Often Confused

lie/lying/lay/have lain-to rest or recline Note: It may be used to describe the position of an object. lay/laying/laid/ have laid-to put	I **lie** on the floor when I am tired. The children are **lying** on the bed. Every evening we **lay** our heads on the pillow. The sleepyheads **have lain** on the couch a long time. **Lay** those pears down. We are **laying** the papers on the table. Yesterday, we **laid** the papers on the table. Where have you **laid** the papers?
leave-to go away let- to allow or permit	We need to **leave** on time for piano class. **Let** him do it on his own.
loose- opposite of tight lose- suffer loss	The **loose** sweater did not fit. I hope you don't **lose** the game.
"I" verses "me" Hint: Remove the other person from the sentence to see which sounds correct. Myself	Jennifer and **I** went to the party. Give the books to Jake and **me**. **I, myself** have an opportunity to give grace. **I** thought to **myself**, "This is wonderful!"
passed-(verb) past tense of pass past-(noun) history past-(adjective) former past-(preposition) farther than	We **passed** their car on the road. Her **past** piano teacher said she was ready for the next level. He went **past** the library.
Presence-(noun) state of being Presents-(plural) gift	Your **presence** in our home is a blessing. We have **presents** for you.
principle- important or main fact principal-the head of a school or business	The **principle** is work diligently. The **principal** is my pal.
rise/rising/rose/have risen-to go up raise/raising/raised/have raised-to move something up	I **rise** early in the morning. I am **rising** early tomorrow. The rocket **rose** beyond our sight. He has **risen** indeed! I will **raise** the blinds on the window. **Raising** your own food is satisfying. The store **raised** the prices. You have **raised** a great question.
shone-(verb, past tense of shine) shown-(verb, past participle of show) to reveal	The stars **shone** brightly over the prairie. She has **shown** me her art work.

Words Often Confused

Since-(preposition, conjunction, and adjective) from time past Sense-ability to hear, smell, taste, touch, see, or perceive.	**_Since_** the dawn of time, man has told stories. The dog has a keen **_sense_** of smell.
sit/sitting/sat/have sat- to rest set/setting/have set-to put	**_Sit_** down on the comfy chair. I **_sat_** down on the couch. We **_have sat_** down, and we don't care to get up. **_Set_** the tea on the table. I am **_setting_** the tea on the table. I **_have set_** the cups next to the teapot.
stationary-in a fixed place stationery- writing paper	The price of the land remained **_stationary_**. I love the **_stationery_** you used to write the note.
than-comparison then- refers to time	I love you more **_than_** chocolate. It was **_then_** I realized my love for chocolate.
their-belonging to a group there-a place they're-(contraction) they are there's-(contraction) there is	**_Their_** socks are red and white. **_There_** are three dogs. **_They're_** ready for Christmas. **_There's_** one thing I must do before I go to sleep.
threw-to throw through-in one side and out the other	He **_threw_** the ball. She went **_through_** the tunnel.
to-direction too-more two-number	I skipped **_to_** the pool I ate **_too_** much candy. I ate **_two_** pieces of candy.
waist- the middle of the body waste- to expend carelessly	The dress doesn't seem to fit at the **_waist_**. It is sad to **_waste_** all that food.
weak-lacking strength week- seven days	After his accident, he was very **_weak_**. There are seven days in one **_week._**
weather-atmospheric conditions whether-doubt	The **_weather_** is beautiful today. I am not sure **_whether_** or not I will be going tomorrow.
which-refers to *things* Use "which" if the information that follows is **not needed** to communicate the idea of the sentence. It has less information but will still be a sentence. that-refers to *people or things* Use "that" if the information that follows is **needed** to communicate the idea of the sentence.	I attended a conference, **_which ended on Saturday._** I returned the book **_that I borrowed from the library._**

LH
27

Words Often Confused

who's-(contraction) who is whose-possessive of who	**Who's** coming to dinner? **Whose** bicycle is in the driveway?
your-belonging to another you're-(contraction) you are	**Your** ice cream was made with the finest ingredients. **You're** a great chef!

Writing Formats

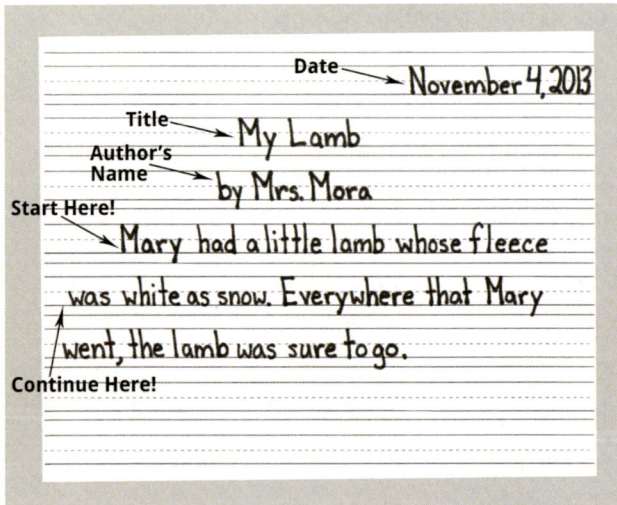

Younger Student Essay Format

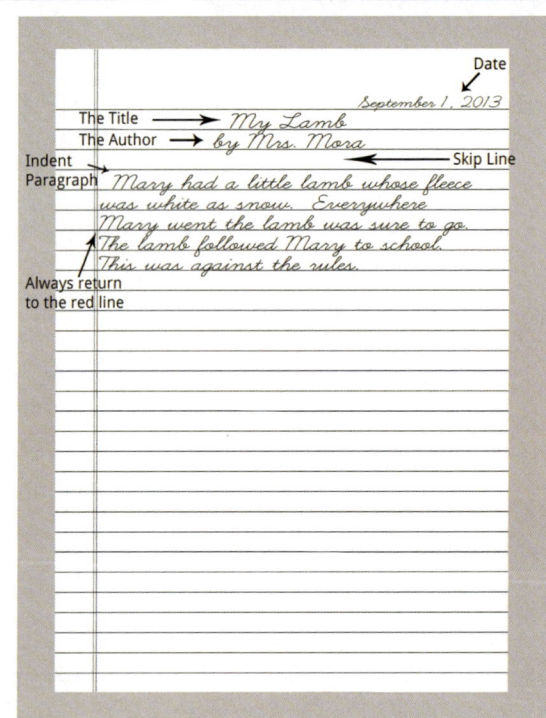

Older Student Essay Format

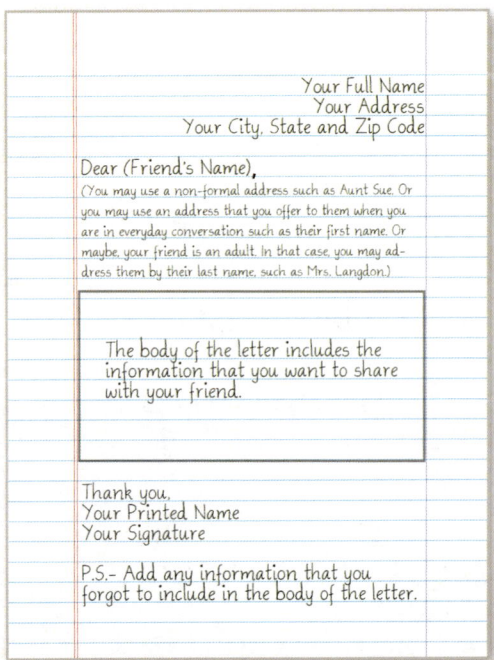

Friendly Letter Format

Business Letter Format

Plural Rules- More Than One

If the noun ends with a consonant followed by a "y", drop the "y" and add "ies"	berry—berries activity—activities butterfly—butterflies pony—ponies spy—spies penny—pennies
If the noun ends in: -ch and does not say the "k" sound -s -sh -x -z add "es"	church—churches bus—buses dish—dishes fox—foxes waltz—waltzes
If the noun ends in "ch" and says the "k" sound add "s".	stomach—stomachs epoch—epochs monarch—monarchs
If the noun ends in a "f" or "fe", drop it and add "ves".	half—halves knife—knives
If the noun ends in two vowels followed by "f" add "s".	chief—chiefs spoof—spoofs
If the noun ends in a vowel followed by "o" add "s".	zoo—zoos ratio—ratios video—videos
If the noun ends with a consonant followed by "o", add "s" or "es". Example #1 :Most nouns that end in "o", add "s" Example #1 : Many of these nouns can be spelled either way. Example #3 : Some of these nouns are only spelled correctly if you add "es" When in doubt, look it up!	Example #1 solo—solos avocado—avocados Example#2 banjo—banjos—banjoes volcano—volcanos—volcanoes Example #3 domino—dominoes potato—potatoes hero—heroes

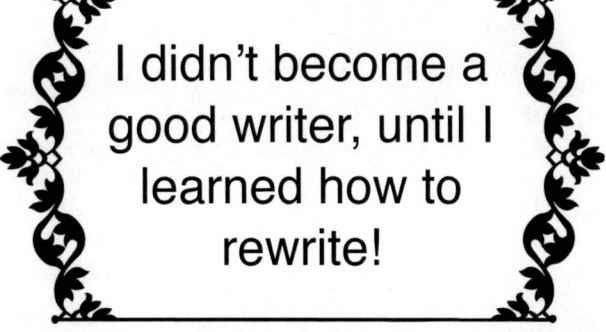

I didn't become a good writer, until I learned how to rewrite!

Subject-Verb Agreement

Subjects and Verbs MUST agree!
Single subjects take a single verb.
Plural subjects take plural verbs.

1. Find the subject of the sentence.
2. Find the verb or action word of the sentence.
3. Make sure they match.
4. Sometimes subject-verb agreements can be tricky. If you are not sure, look it up in a dictionary.

Verbs that show "being"
I : am, was, have been
you : are, were, have been
he, she, or it: is, was, has been
we: are, were, have been
you: are, were, have been
they: are, were, have been

23 Helping Verbs
The "Beings"-**is, am, are, was, were**
The "Bs" -**be, been, being**
The "Hs"-**has, had, have**
The "D's" -**do does, did**
The "oulds"-**could, would, should**
The "Ms"- **may, might, must**
"The last ones"-**will, can, shall**

Verb Tense Definitions

The **tense** of the verb shows the **time of the action**. In writing, it is important to make your verb tenses match or agree. This chart shows the different tenses of the verb, "to give".

Verb Tense	Singular	Plural
Present Tense The action is happening now.	I give you give he, she, or it gives	we give you give they give
Past Tense The action happened in the past.	I gave you gave he, she, or it gave	we gave you gave they gave
Future Tense Th action will happen in the future.	I will (shall) give you will give he, she, or it will give	we will (shall) give you will give they will give
Present Perfect Tense The action was completed prior to the present.	I have given you have given he, she, or it has given	we have given you have given they have given
Past Perfect Tense The action was completed before another action.	I had given you had given he, she, or it had given	we had given you had given they had given
Future Perfect Tense Shows when a future action will be completed.	I will (shall) have given you will have given he, she, or it will have given	we will have given you will have given they will have given

Irregular Verbs - Frequently Misused

Verb	Present Participle	Past	Past Participle
begin	is beginning	began	have begun
blow	is blowing	blew	have blown
break	is breaking	broke	have broken
bring	is bringing	brought	have brought
burst	is bursting	burst	have burst
choose	is choosing	chose	have chosen
come	is coming	came	have come
dive	is diving	dove	have dived
do	is doing	did	have done
drink	is drinking	drank	have drunk
drive	is driving	drove	have driven
eat	is eating	ate	have eaten
fall	is falling	fell	have fallen
freeze	is freezing	froze	have frozen
give	is giving	gave	have given
go	is going	went	have gone
grow	is growing	grew	have grown
know	is knowing	knew	have known
put	is putting	put	have put
ride	is riding	rode	have ridden
ring	is ringing	rang	have rung
run	is running	ran	have run
see	is seeing	saw	have seen
shake	is shaking	shook	have shaken
shrink	is shrinking	shrank	have shrunk
sink	is sinking	sank	have sunk
speak	is speaking	spoke	have spoken
steal	is stealing	stole	have stolen
sting	is stinging	stung	have stung
strike	is striking	struck	have struck
swear	is swearing	swore	have sworn
swim	is swimming	swam	have swum
take	is taking	took	have taken
tear	is tearing	tore	have torn
throw	is throwing	threw	have thrown
wear	is wearing	wore	have worn
write	is writing	wrote	have written

Grammar Rules for Numbers

Rule Number	Rule	Example
1	Write out numbers 1-9	one, two, three, four, five, six, seven, eight, nine
2	One word numbers-spell out. Two word numbers-write the numeral. Note: Experts don't agree on this rule. Recommend: Be consistent when writing numbers.	*Incorrect*: I have 8 children. *Correct*: I have **eight** children. *Incorrect*: Please buy twenty-four eggs. *Correct*: Please buy **24** eggs.
3	Do not start a sentence with a numeral.	*Incorrect*: 300,000 copies were sold the first day. *Correct*: On the first day, **300,000** copies were sold. *Correct*: **Three hundred thousand** copies were sold the first day.
4	Distinguish two numbers next to each other by writing a numeral (symbol) or spell out the word.	We saw **five 7-year** olds playing games on the lawn. The **first 20** people to register will receive a gift.
5	Write out ordinal numbers.	He is my **first** cousin. She took **second** place in the competition.
6	Be consistent when writing multiple numbers.	*Incorrect*: During the bake sale, the children sold twelve pies, 150 cookies, and 36 brownies. *Correct*: During the bake sale, the children sold 12 pies, 150 cookies, and 36 brownies.
7	Centuries or decades should be spelled out.	Distance running became popular in the **eighties.** In the **fourteenth** century, the Canterbury Tales made its debut.
8	Rounding numbers When rounding numbers, spell out the number. Note: Use numerals only if it is an exact number.	*Incorrect*: About 350,000,000 people speak Spanish. *Correct*: About 350 **million** people speak Spanish.
9	Percentages If a percentage begins a sentence, it should be spelled out.	*Incorrect*: 4% of the school-age population is homeschooled. *Correct*: Four percent of the school-age population is homeschooled.

Parts of Speech

Part of Speech	Definition and a Brief Example
Noun	**A noun is a person, place, thing, or idea** Person: James, Captain Knucklehead, runners... Place: New York, library, Mars... Thing: banana, boat, pyramid... Idea: truth, justice, honesty...
Verb	**A verb is a word that shows action or being** Shows action: jump, ski, pick... Shows being: am, is, was...
Pronoun	**A pronoun is a word used in place of a noun.** Personal pronouns: I, my, mine, me, we, ours, us.... Reflexive pronouns: myself, ourselves... Relative pronouns: who, whom, whose...... Interrogative pronouns: who, which, whose.... Demonstrative pronouns: this, that, these, those...
Adjectives	**A word that describes a noun or pronoun.** Example: I have **five** fingers. Example: I would love to have a **cheese** sandwich. Example: I like **that** shirt. Example: **My** sister is arriving.
Adverbs	**A word that describes a verb, adjective, or adverb.** Example: I am **completely** happy. Example: I will see you **later**.
Conjunctions	**A word that that is used to join words or groups of words.** Example: and, but, or, nor, for, yet, so...
Prepositions	**A preposition is a word to show relationship to a noun or pronoun in the sentence.** Example: about, above, across, after, against, around, at, before, behind, below, beneath, beside, between, beyond, by, down, during, except, for, from, in, inside, into, like, near, of, off, on, out, outside, over, since, through, throughout, till, to, toward, under, until, up, upon, with.......
Interjections	**An interjection is a word that is used to express emotion set apart from the sentence by a comma or exclamation point.** Example: Hey! Ugh! Example: Wow, you are amazing!

Common Literary Techniques

Literary Techniques- The way a writer writes to convey meaning or emotion.

Simile- a comparison between two things that uses "like" or "as"
Example: The light was as bright as the stars.
Example: Her smile was like a rainbow on a cloudy day.

Metaphor- a comparison between two things that does not use the word "like" or "as"
Example: America is a melting pot for the world.
Example: Life is a wild roller coaster ride with ups and downs.

Mood- the way an author uses words to create a feeling
Example: The rays of the sun touched her cheek and awakened her to the new life that was beginning.
Example: He fumbled as he slowly tore the envelope handed to him by his boss. A chill from the window whisked down the empty hall. He slowly read the note that the factory was shutting down tomorrow.

Tone- the way the author uses words to influence the reader about certain ideas or persons
Example: If the author likes the idea of caring for the sick then he/she may have a character in the story that receives deep satisfaction from caring for the sick.
Example: If the author has respect for the office of presidency, he/she will use respectful words when speaking about the president.

Symbolism- an author may use an object to represent a truth or an idea
Example: In *Lord of the Rings*, the ring symbolizes the temptation of man and that one needs to remain humble to conquer its power.

Hyperbole- an exaggeration that helps make the authors point
Example: Paul Bunyan was as big as an ox and could swing a redwood tree like an axe.

Irony- words that have opposite literal meaning that makes the reader laugh or think about the truth.
Example: The dentist broke his tooth biting into a piece of hard candy.

Onomatopoeia- words used to describe a sound
Example: The screeching car zoomed past our family.
Example: "Meow," said the cat.

Personification- an author may give human qualities to an object or animal
Example: The clouds began to cry on that dreary day.
Example: Knucklehead's sense of responsibility to save the day kicked into high gear!

Alliteration- words that use the same beginning letter
Example: The sly snake slithered across the desert.

Foreshadowing- an author gives hints about what is going to happen in the story
Example: In the story, "Little Red Riding Hood", Little Red Riding Hood is not listening to her mother explain about the danger of strangers.

Flashback- an author shows the reader the end of the story first and then continues the story
Example: In the beginning of the story, the hero is hanging from a cliff. The story continues with a description of the events that led to the hero hanging from a cliff.

Sentence Types and Structure

Sentence Type	Example
Statement-Declarative (Makes a statement)	The cat is sitting next to the window. (ends with a period)
Question-Interrogative (Asks a question)	Is the cat sitting next to the window? (ends with a question mark)
Command- Imperative (Tells someone to do something)	(you is understood) Sit by the window with the cat. (Ends in a period or exclamation point)
Exclamation- Exclamatory (Shows strong emotion)	Help, the cat is falling from the window! (ends with an exclamation point)
Simple Sentence (Subject + Verb)	I drink milk.
Compound Sentence (subject+verb + and+ subject +verb) and/or/but/nor/or/so/yet	Sally whispered to her sister, and she smiled.
Introductory Participle Phrase (Describes a noun or pronoun)	Walking rapidly, we reached the park in time for the game.
Appositive Phrase (Renames the noun)	Jennifer, the girl next door, is thoughtful.
Introductory Prepositional Phrase	With a paintbrush in hand, Mark began to paint.
Introductory Adverb Clause	After Kyle had completed his writing, he gave it to the publisher.

> I love all the different types of sentences! I want to use them all!

Paragraph Editing Checklist for Second Rough Draft

Did the writer stay on task with the writing project?
Is there an interesting attention-getter sentence?
Is there a closing sentence that restates the main idea using different words?
Do all the sentences in the middle of the paragraph support the main idea?
Are there transitional words to help connect ideas?
Is each sentence clear and complete? Identify the weakest sentence and remove it or fix it.
Are there fragments? A fragment is an incomplete sentence.
Are there run-on sentences? A run-on sentence is when two or more complete sentences are joined incorrectly.
Are there dangling modifiers? A dangling modifier is a word or word phrase that is confusing .
Were different types of sentences used?
Do all the subjects and verbs agree?
Are the verb tenses consistent? Example: past, present, and future
Are all the "dead words" removed?
Are there literary techniques such as similes or metaphors?
Are all the words spelled correctly?
Is the punctuation correct?
Is the paragraph indented?

Use for your yearly writing portfolio
© Here To Help Learning • Reproduction prohibited • Flight 2 Launching Paragraph Writing

Purpose in Writing

And whatever you do, whether in **_word_** or deed, do it all in the name of the Lord Jesus, giving thanks to God the Father through him.

Colossians 3:17

The Writing Process — Oh The Places I've Been

Brainstorm	
Make a List	
Webbing	
First Rough Draft	
First Input (Content Focus)	
Second Rough Draft	
Second Input (Grammar & Spelling Focus)	
Final Recopy	
Publish	

© Here To Help Learning • Reproduction prohibited • Flight 2 Launching Paragraph Writing Lesson 1

Take Off — Game

Sentence — 👍
👎 No Sentence

A sentence has a complete thought.
It has a noun (person, place or thing) and a verb (an action word).

To Play: Put your thumbs up if it is a sentence.

Example:
Simon and Joseph went to the library.

Put your thumbs down if it is NOT a sentence.

Examples:
Went to the library. (Noun missing)

Simon and Joseph. (Verb missing)

Round 1 — **Teacher** offers sentences and phrases for the students to judge.

Round 2 — **Students take turns** offering sentences and phrases for the other students to judge.

Round 3 — **Teacher offers phrases** and student must fix them.

© Here To Help Learning • Reproduction prohibited • Flight 2 Launching Paragraph Writing Lesson 1

Take Off

Writing Warm-up

Name _____

Word Box

Look at the picture. Choose 6 words that describe the picture. Write the words in the boxes. Use them in a sentence or create a story.

© Here To Help Learning • Reproduction prohibited • Flight 2 Launching Paragraph Writing Lesson 1

Full Throttle
Brainstorm Worksheet

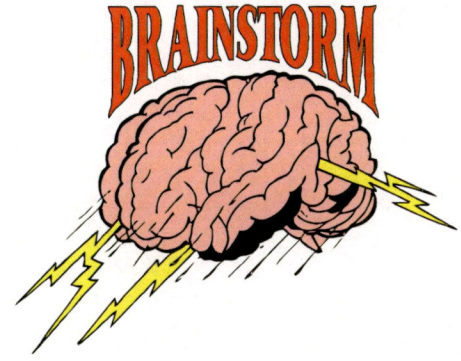

After brainstorming, the place I have visited that I would like to write about is_____.

Take Off

Writing Warm-up

Name_____

Word Box

Look at the picture. Choose 6 words that describe the picture. Write the words in the boxes. Use them in a sentence or create a story.

Full Throttle

Make a List!

Project name: Oh, The Places I've Been

Directions: Make a list of how you would describe the place you have visited. Be sure to use all five of your senses: seeing, hearing, smelling, tasting, and touching.

1. _____

2. _____

3. _____

4. _____

5. _____

6. _____

7. _____

8. _____

9. _____

10. _____

© Here To Help Learning • Reproduction prohibited • Flight 2 Launching Paragraph Writing Lesson 2

Take Off

Writing Warm-up

Name_____

Word Box

Look at the picture. Choose 6 words that describe the picture. Write the words in the boxes. Use them in a sentence or create a story.

© Here To Help Learning • Reproduction prohibited • Flight 2 Launching Paragraph Writing Lesson 3

Full Throttle

Webbing

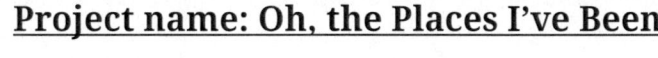

Project name: Oh, the Places I've Been

Directions: Look at your list from last week. Group like ideas into the unshaded ovals. Do not use the shaded ovals this week. Next lesson, you will learn how to write a fabulous attention-getter sentence for the first shaded oval and how to write a wonderful closing sentence for last shaded oval.

Attention-Getter Sentence

Beginning

Middle

End

Closing Sentence

© Here To Help Learning • Reproduction prohibited • Flight 2 Launching Paragraph Writing Lesson 3

Take Off
Writing Warm-up

Name_____

Word Box
Look at the picture. Choose 6 words that describe the picture. Write the words in the boxes. Use them in a sentence or create a story.

© Here To Help Learning • Reproduction prohibited • Flight 2 Launching Paragraph Writing Lesson 4

Full Throttle

I Can Help! First Input

Project name: Oh, The Places I've Been

Name of Student Presenting: _____

Input Questions	Yes	No	More Please!	Not Needed
Is there an attention-getting sentence?				
Is there a closing sentence?				
Do the sentences flow together?				
Is there enough content?				
Are there transitional words?				
Does the author stay on task with the project instructions?				
🎨 Are there words that help the reader see?				
🎨 Are there words that help the reader hear?				
🎨 Are there words that help the reader feel?				
🎨 Are there words that help the reader smell?				
🎨 Are there words that help the reader taste?				

Praise-

Input-

Praise-

Change these DEAD WORDS:

_____

_____

_____

For instructions on how to change a dead word, see the Language Helps Booklet.

© Here To Help Learning • Permission to copy page • Flight 2 Launching Paragraph Writing Lesson 5

Making an Essay Folder

Step 1. Create your Essay Folder.

1. Gather Supplies
   - 12"X18" construction paper- any color
   - Long arm stapler
   - 5-6 copies of lined paper.

2. Fold construction paper in half widthwise.

3. Place 5-6 copies of lined paper on the lower half of the folded construction paper. Using a long arm stapler, staple the top of the lined paper to the construction paper.

4. Fold the construction paper back over the lined paper. Using a glue stick, attach the cover to the front of the essay folder.

Step 2. Use the lesson cover template on the next page.

Ideas:
Decorate the cover with pictures from your story.
Use borders and color in the background.
Be creative!

Sample Essay Folder Cover For This Project

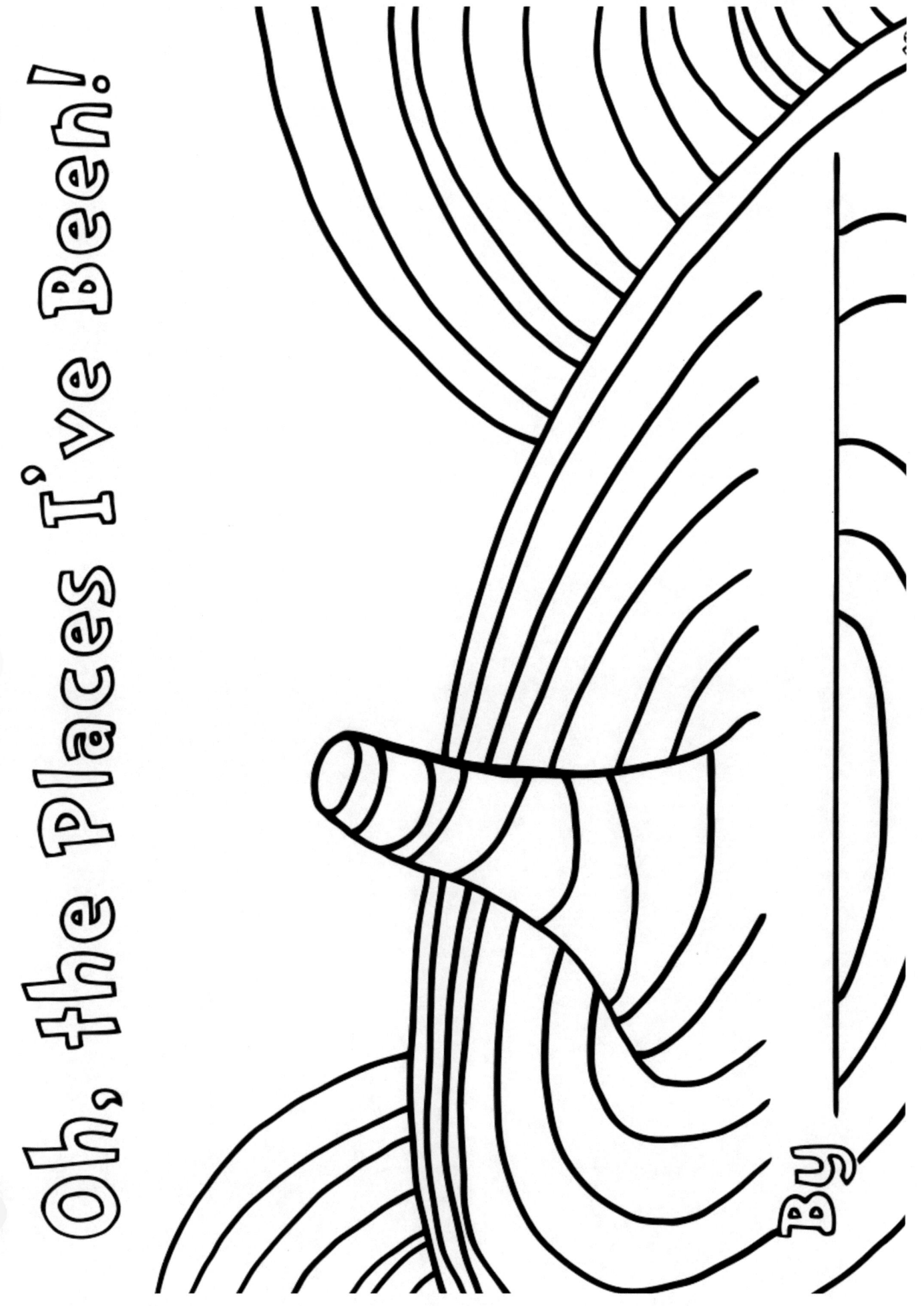

The Writing Process — Potato People

Brainstorm	
Make a List	
Webbing	
First Rough Draft	
First Input (Content Focus)	
Second Rough Draft	
Second Input (Grammar & Spelling Focus)	
Final Recopy	
Publish	

Take Off
Game

DEAD WORDS TELL NO TALES

Dead words are over-used words that do not give clear, crisp descriptions.

To Play:
- Break group into teams (no more than 2-3 students in group)
- Set timer for two minutes.
- Teacher announces "The dead word for today is..." (pause for dramatic effect) and announces the dead word for the day.
- Students write the word on the tombstone.
- Teacher says, "Go!" Students come up with as many descriptive words as possible and write them on the flowers. When the timer goes off, students return.
- As a group, evaluate the entries. The team that has the most descriptive words receives an extra "Discovery Ticket."

Potato People

Sometimes writers use their imaginations to create characters for a story. Sometimes they will create their character by drawing a picture, sculpting clay or decorating an object. It is a type of brainstorming called modeling. Modeling helps a writer see the character. We are going to use this type of brainstorming in our new project called, Potato People.

Supplies: Potato, assorted craft supplies (Be creative!), straight pins
Directions: Create face, hair, clothes, and hat using craft supplies. Pin them to your potato.

Here are some student examples of "Potato People" that were written by second graders. I am proud that these students are learning to write and apply the writing process! There is always plenty of room to grow!

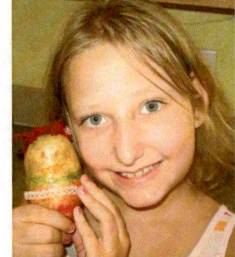

Exciting Day with Elizabeth by: Hannah M.

Come to the country with Elizabeth. Elizabeth is nine years old, and she has lots of freckles on her face. Elizabeth likes to ride her white and brown horse named Penny down by the old fishing pond. Before Elizabeth rides her horse, she puts Penny's long chili-colored hair in a ponytail. Elizabeth has aquamarine eyes that sparkle in the sun. When Elizabeth is not riding her horse Penny, she likes to bebop on her tire swing. On hot summer days, Elizabeth likes to swim in her swimming pool. Elizabeth has a kitten named Snowbell. Snowbell is a fluffy, white kitten with brown ears, brown paws and a brown tip on her tail. Elizabeth likes to sew fancy clothes for Snowbell. Elizabeth's favorite dress for Snowbell is pink and yellow with a blue flower on the side. They dress up together and have tea parties. When days are slow in the country, Elizabeth likes to sit back and read the Chronicles of Narnia adventure books. At night, Elizabeth tucks Snowbell into her kitten bed and tucks herself in bed. Elizabeth falls asleep quickly. What a way to end the day!

Lazy Luigi by Logan H.

The best potato I ever met was Luigi Tatermater. He is an incredible potato person! I want to tell you about him. Luigi is twenty-five years old. He wears his GI Joe shirt every single day. He talks in a squeaky voice. "Hello! I'm Luigi," he says. He wears a hat to keep the sun off his head because he is allergic to the sun. He also hates doing yard work because he doesn't like being sweaty. He is round and fat. In fact, Luigi is so round he doesn't walk, he wobbles. Luigi is unbeatable at Super Mario Brothers because he plays Wii for twenty hours every day. I bet he's tired! Luigi likes to make cars. He wants to be an engineer when he grows up. His favorite color is camo. Luigi eats a lot but never mashed potatoes! Do you like my friend Luigi? I think he's totally cool!

What will yours look like?

© Here To Help Learning • Reproduction prohibited • Flight 2 Launching Paragraph Writing Lesson 7

Flying Solo

Make A List Worksheet

Project name: Potato People

Directions: Complete the chart below. Write down anything else you want your readers to know about this character on the back of this paper. Be as detailed as possible.

What is your potato person's name and age?	
How does he/she talk?	
How does he/she walk?	
What are his/her favorite things to do?	
What are things he/she does NOT like to do?	
What is his/her favorite color?	
What does he/she want to be when he/she grows up?	
Add something…	
Add something…	

Student Writing Evaluation

Name _____ Writing Project: <u>Oh, The Places I've Been</u>

My best sentence was _____

_____

_____

I like this sentence because _____

_____

_____

I could improve my writing on my next project by _____

_____

_____

_____ Yes, I published my project

Parent Note:

Co-Op Teachers Note:

Take Off
Game

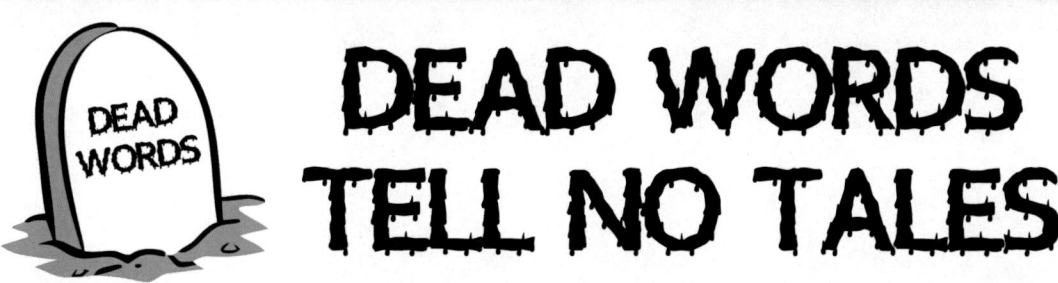

DEAD WORDS TELL NO TALES

Dead words are over-used words that do not give clear, crisp descriptions.

To Play:
- Break group into teams (no more than 2-3 students in group)
- Set timer for two minutes.
- Teacher announces "The dead word for today is..." (pause for dramatic effect) and announces the dead word for the day.
- Students write the word on the tombstone.
- Teacher says, "Go!" Students come up with as many descriptive words as possible and write them on the flowers. When the timer goes off, students return.
- As a group, evaluate the entries. The team that has the most descriptive words receives an extra "Discovery Ticket."

© Here To Help Learning • Reproduction prohibited • Flight 2 Launching Paragraph Writing Lesson 8

Take Off

Writing Warm-up

Name _____

Word Box

Look at the picture. Choose 6 words that describe the picture. Write the words in the boxes. Use them in a sentence or create a story.

© Here To Help Learning • Reproduction prohibited • Flight 2 Launching Paragraph Writing Lesson 8

Full Throttle

Webbing

Project name: Potato People

Directions: Look at your list from last lesson and group like ideas into the three unshaded ovals. In the top shaded oval, write a fabulous attention-getter sentence and in the last shaded oval, add a wonderful closing sentence. Remember, you do not have to use all of your list items.

- **Attention-Getter Sentence**
- **What does your potato person look like?**
- **What does your potato person act like?**
- **What does your potato person like to do?**
- **Closing Sentence**

© Here To Help Learning • Reproduction prohibited • Flight 2 Launching Paragraph Writing Lesson 8

Take Off

Game

DEAD WORDS TELL NO TALES

Dead words are over-used words that do not give clear, crisp descriptions.

To Play:
- Break group into teams (no more than 2-3 students in group)
- Set timer for two minutes.
- Teacher announces "The dead word for today is..." (pause for dramatic effect) and announces the dead word for the day.
- Students write the word on the tombstone.
- Teacher says, "Go!" Students come up with as many descriptive words as possible and write them on the flowers. When the timer goes off, students return.
- As a group, evaluate the entries. The team that has the most descriptive words receives an extra "Discovery Ticket."

© Here To Help Learning • Reproduction prohibited • Flight 2 Launching Paragraph Writing Lesson 9

Take Off

Writing Warm-up

Name_____

Word Box

Look at the picture. Choose 6 words that describe the picture. Write the words in the boxes. Use them in a sentence or create a story.

© Here To Help Learning • Reproduction prohibited • Flight 2 Launching Paragraph Writing Lesson 9

Full Throttle

I Can Help! First Input

Project name: Potato People

Name of Student Presenting: _____

Input Questions	Yes	No	More Please!	Not Needed
Is there an attention-getting sentence?				
Is there a closing sentence?				
Do the sentences flow together?				
Is there enough content?				
Are there transitional words?				
Does the author stay on task with the project instructions?				
🎨 Are there words that help the reader see?				
🎨 Are there words that help the reader hear?				
🎨 Are there words that help the reader feel?				
🎨 Are there words that help the reader smell?				
🎨 Are there words that help the reader taste?				

Praise-

Input-

Praise-

Change these DEAD WORDS:

_____
_____
_____

For instructions on how to change a dead word, see the Language Helps Booklet.

Making an Essay Folder

Step 1. *Create your Essay Folder.*

1. Gather Supplies
  - 12"X18" construction paper- any color
  - Long arm stapler
  - 5-6 copies of lined paper.

2. Fold construction paper in half widthwise.

3. Place 5-6 copies of lined paper on the lower half of the folded construction paper. Using a long arm stapler, staple the top of the lined paper to the construction paper.

4. Fold the construction paper back over the lined paper. Using a glue stick, attach the cover to the front of the essay folder.

Step 2. *Use the lesson cover template on the next page.*

Ideas:
Decorate the cover with pictures from your story.
Use borders and color in the background.
Be creative!

Sample Essay Folder Cover For This Project

LITTLE HELP

Writing Project 3

© Here To Help Learning • Reproduction prohibited • Flight 2 Launching Paragraph Writing

The Writing Process — Little Help

Brainstorm	
Make a List	
Webbing & Organizing	
First Rough Draft **Content- Plot & Character**	
First Input **Plot & Character**	
First Rough Draft **Content- Setting and Conflict**	
First Input **Setting and Conflict**	
Second Rough Draft **Revision**	
Second Input **Revision**	
Recopy	
Publish	

Take Off
Game

Make a Noun Do Anything!

A <u>noun</u> is a person, place or thing.
A <u>verb</u> is an action word.

Directions:
1. Add a verb or verb phrase to the nouns below.
2. Use both words in a sentence.
3. If you are able, complete challenges #1 and #2.
4. You may write a sentence or draw a picture.

Remember: It's okay to be silly, just make sure it's God-honoring.

Example: The ball sang.

LA LA LA LA LA!

Challenge #1: Add **colorful words** to describe the **noun**.
   Example: The **perfumed ball** sang.

Challenge #2: Add **colorful words** to describe the **verbs**.
   Example: The perfumed ball **sang with a mousy voice**.

Noun	Add a Verb
 (car)	
 (teddy bear)	
 (balloon)	

© Here To Help Learning • Reproduction prohibited • Flight 2 Launching Paragraph Writing Lesson 12

Take Off

Writing Warm-up

Name_____

Word Box

Look at the picture. Choose 6 words that describe the picture. Write the words in the boxes. Use them in a sentence or create a story.

© Here To Help Learning • Reproduction prohibited • Flight 2 Launching Paragraph Writing Lesson 12

Full Throttle

There are a lot of problems and unfairness in the world. God asks us to help right these wrongs. For example, there are a lot of scriptures where God asks us to help the widows and orphans. There are scriptures that tell us to encourage the brokenhearted and to feed the poor. God's word also tells us to share the good news of Christ. However, it is hard to make a difference in the world when you are the only one working to solve a problem. God wants us to work together.

1 Corinthians 12:12-25 (New American Standard Bible)

For even as the body is one and yet has many members, and all the members of the body, though they are many, are one body, so also is Christ. For by one Spirit we were all baptized into one body, whether Jews or Greeks, whether slaves or free, and we were all made to drink of one Spirit.

For the body is not one member, but many. If the foot says, "Because I am not a hand, I am not a part of the body," it is not for this reason any the less a part of the body. And if the ear says, "Because I am not an eye, I am not a part of the body," it is not for this reason any the less a part of the body. If the whole body were an eye, where would the hearing be? If the whole were hearing, where would the sense of smell be? But now God has placed the members, each one of them, in the body, just as He desired. If they were all one member, where would the body be? But now there are many members, but one body. And the eye cannot say to the hand, "I have no need of you"; or again the head to the feet, "I have no need of you." On the contrary, it is much truer that the members of the body which seem to be weaker are necessary; and those members of the body which we deem less honorable, on these we bestow more abundant honor, and our less presentable members become much more presentable, whereas our more presentable members have no need of it. But God has so composed the body, giving more abundant honor to that member which lacked, so that there may be no division in the body, but that the members may have the same care for one another.

There are many people that come together to help those in need. Most of them will say, they could use some extra help. If other people knew about them and what they do, maybe they would offer a little help. We will learn to write in such a way that our reader will want to help. It is called persuasive writing. We will give our readers the information about the organization and then we will ask our readers to help.

Full Throttle
Brainstorm Worksheet

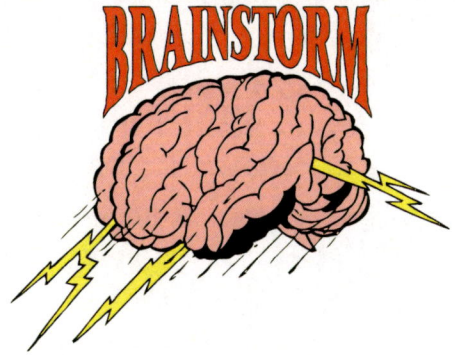

Project Name: Little Help

Let's brainstorm about organizations in your church, community, or around the world that need a "Little Help".

After brainstorming together, there is a group that can use a little help.

It is called _____.

Make A List Worksheet

Project name: Little Help

Directions: Make a list of the important facts about the group you have chosen. You will have to do some research. When we research, we ask the 5 "W" questions plus the question how. Ask your parents for help to search for information or "knowledge nuggets".

Who? What is the name of the organization?	
What? What do they do to help?	
Where? Where do they go to help?	
When? When do they help others? Example: Once a year, every week…	
Why? Why do they help?	
How? How can someone help this organization?	
Other information	
Other information	
Other information	

© Here To Help Learning • Reproduction prohibited • Flight 2 Launching Paragraph Writing Lesson 12

Student Writing Evaluation

Name _____   Writing Project: <u>Potato People</u>

My best sentence was _____

_____

_____

I like this sentence because _____

_____

_____

I could improve my writing on my next project by _____

_____

_____

_____ Yes, I published my project

Parent Note:

Co-Op Teachers Note:

Take Off
Game

Make a Noun Do Anything!

A <u>noun</u> is a person, place or thing.
A <u>verb</u> is an action word.

Directions:
1. Add a verb or verb phrase to the nouns below.
2. Use both words in a sentence.
3. If you are able, complete challenges #1 and #2.
4. You may write a sentence or draw a picture.

Remember: It's okay to be silly, just make sure it's God-honoring.

Example: The ball sang.

Challenge #1: Add **colorful words** to describe the **noun**.
   Example: The **perfumed** **ball** sang.

Challenge #2: Add **colorful words** to describe the **verbs**.
   Example: The perfumed ball **sang with a mousy voice**.

Noun	Add a Verb
🔥 (campfire)	
🧭 (compass)	
⚙️ (wheel)	

© Here To Help Learning • Reproduction prohibited • Flight 2 Launching Paragraph Writing Lesson 13

Take Off

Writing Warm-up

Name_____

Word Box

Look at the picture. Choose 6 words that describe the picture. Write the words in the boxes. Use them in a sentence or create a story.

© Here To Help Learning • Reproduction prohibited • Flight 2 Launching Paragraph Writing Lesson 13

Full Throttle

Webbing

Project name: Little Help

Directions: Look at your list from last week. Group like ideas into the three shaded ovals. In the top shaded oval, write a fabulous attention-getter sentence and in the last shaded oval, add a wonderful closing sentence. Choose the information that you think is most important for your readers to know.

- **Attention-Getter Sentence**
- **Who-What-Where**
- **Why**
- **How can someone help?**
- **Closing Sentence**

Take Off

Writing Warm-up

Make a Noun Do Anything!

A <u>noun</u> is a person, place or thing.
A <u>verb</u> is an action word.

Directions:
1. Add a verb or verb phrase to the nouns below.
2. Use both words in a sentence.
3. If you are able, complete challenges #1 and #2.
4. You may write a sentence or draw a picture.

Remember: It's okay to be silly, just make sure it's God-honoring.

Example: The ball sang.

Challenge #1: Add **colorful words** to describe the **noun**.
   Example: The **perfumed ball** sang.

Challenge #2: Add **colorful words** to describe the **verbs**.
   Example: The perfumed ball **sang with a mousy voice**.

Noun	Add a Verb
🏠	
⛵	
🪄	

© Here To Help Learning • Reproduction prohibited • Flight 2 Launching Paragraph Writing Lesson 14

Take Off

Writing Warm-up

Name _____

Word Box

Look at the picture. Choose 6 words that describe the picture. Write the words in the boxes. Use them in a sentence or create a story.

© Here To Help Learning • Permission to copy page • Flight 2 Launching Paragraph Writing Lesson 14

Full Throttle

I Can Help! First Input

Project name: Little Help

Name of Student Presenting: _____

Input Questions	Yes	No	More Please!	Not Needed
Is there an attention-getting sentence?				
Is there a closing sentence?				
Do the sentences flow together?				
Is there enough content?				
Are there transitional words?				
Does the author stay on task with the project instructions?				
Are there words that help the reader see?				
Are there words that help the reader hear?				
Are there words that help the reader feel?				
Are there words that help the reader smell?				
Are there words that help the reader taste?				

Praise-

Input-

Praise-

Change these DEAD WORDS:

_____

_____

_____

For instructions on how to change a dead word, see the Language Helps Booklet.

© Here To Help Learning • Permission to copy page • Flight 2 Launching Paragraph Writing Lesson 15

Making an Essay Folder

Step 1. *Create your Essay Folder.*

1. Gather Supplies
   - 12"X18" construction paper- any color
   - Long arm stapler
   - 5-6 copies of lined paper.

2. Fold construction paper in half widthwise.

3. Place 5-6 copies of lined paper on the lower half of the folded construction paper. Using a long arm stapler, staple the top of the lined paper to the construction paper.

4. Fold the construction paper back over the lined paper. Using a glue stick, attach the cover to the front of the essay folder.

Step 2. *Use the lesson cover template on the next page.*

Ideas:
Decorate the cover with pictures from your story.
Use borders and color in the background.
Be creative!

Sample Essay Folder Cover For This Project

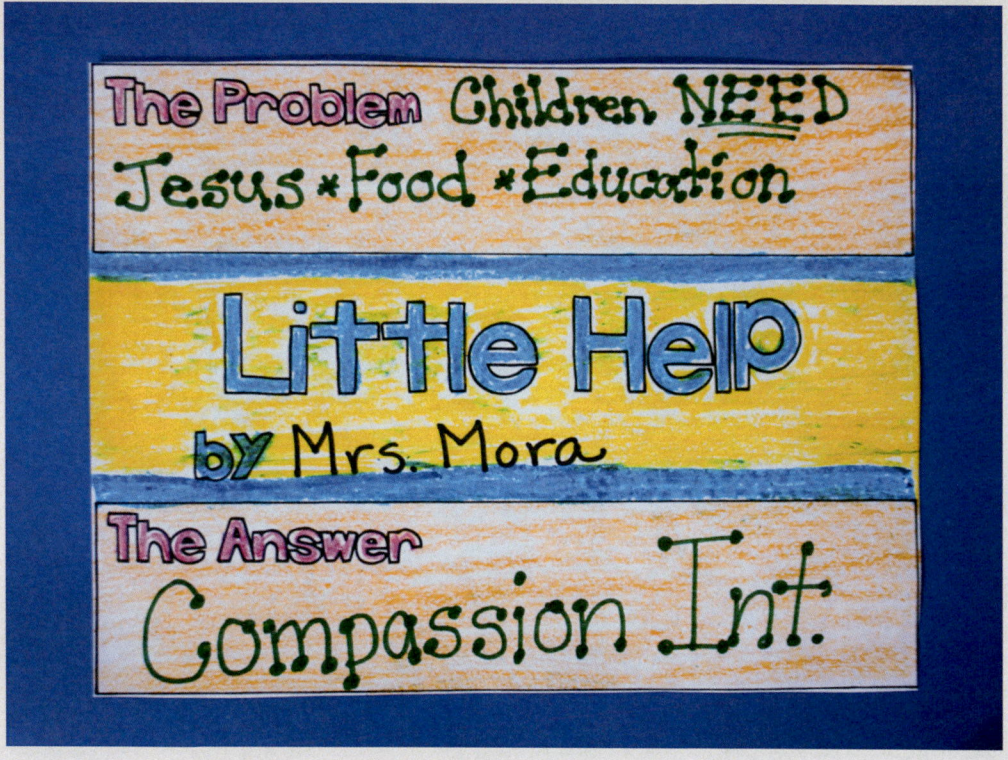

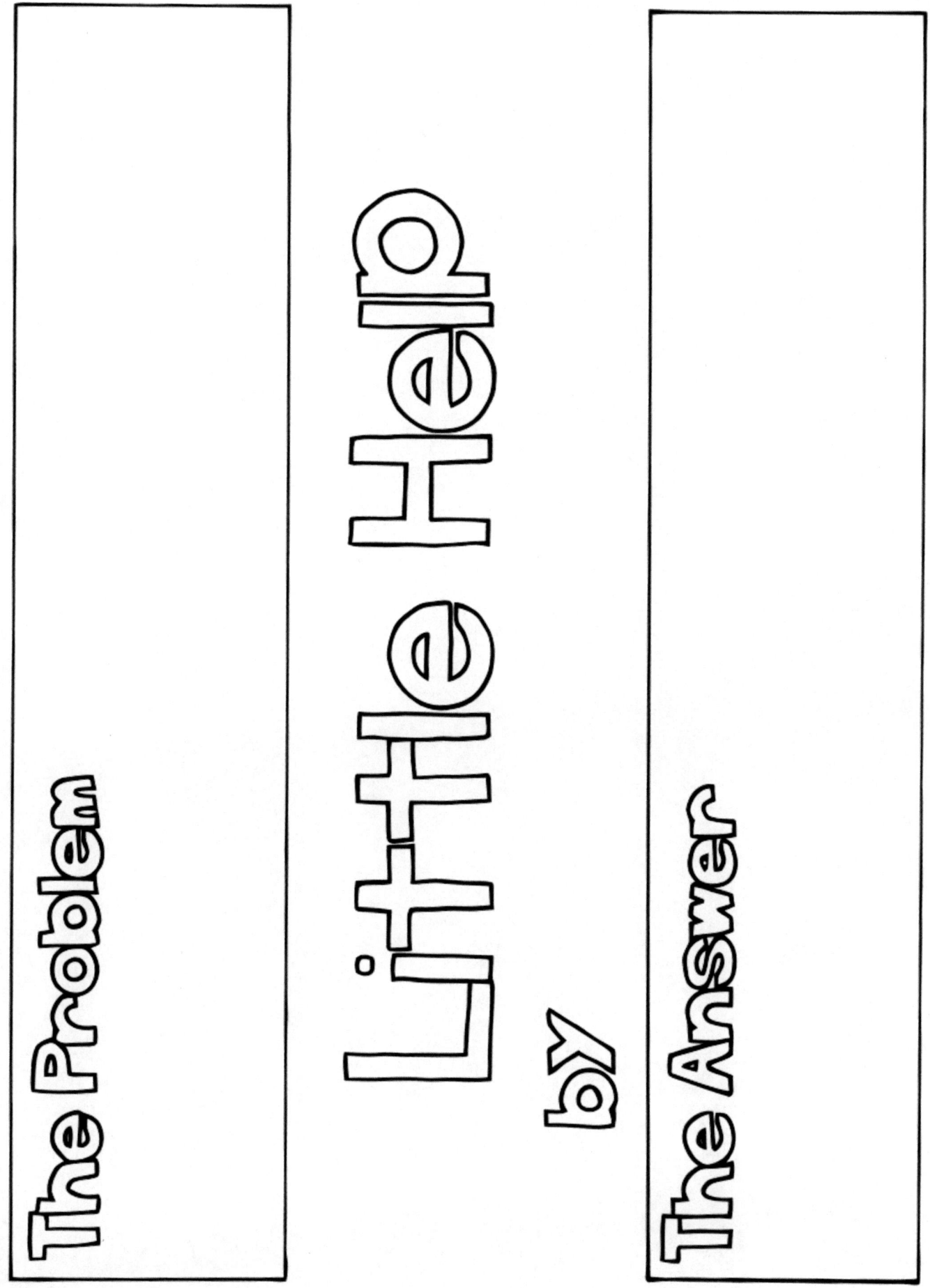

Student Writing Evaluation

Name _____ Writing Project: <u>Little Help</u>

My best sentence was _____

_____

_____

I like this sentence because _____

_____

_____

I could improve my writing on my next project by _____

_____

_____

_____ Yes, I published my project

Parent Note:

Co-Op Teachers Note:

Take Off

Evaluating Poetry with the Three "R"s

When evaluating poetry, just remember the three "R"s!

Rhyme is a repetition of similar sounds of one or more words.
A poem does not have to rhyme to be a poem. However, a poet will choose to rhyme words to create a feeling or to tie ideas together. With rhyming words, a poet can create all types of rhyming patterns.

Example of rhyming words: king and thing

Rhythm is a pattern of regular beats or accents.
You are probably most familiar with rhythms in songs. Drums are often used to create a rhythm in a song. However, every songwriter knows that he must choose words to match the rhythm. Every word has a set number of beats or accents created by syllables. A poem does not have to have a predictable rhythm to be a poem. However, a poet will choose words carefully to create a rhythm that matches the feeling they want their readers to feel.

Example: If a poet wants to write a poem about a battle, he or she may choose words that have a strong beat that sounds like a soldier marching.

Reason is why the poem was written and its meaning.
Every author has a reason for writing a poem. To discover the author's reason, ask yourself these questions:

Why did the author write the poem?
What does he/she want me to know about the subject?
What ideas are being discussed?

Take Off

Three Grammar Rules for Poetry to Remember

1. Capitalize the first word of every line.
Directions: With a yellow crayon, color the first letter on each line of the poem.

God is Amazing
By Tiffany

Oh amazing God!
Oh how kind He is to me!
So mighty and strong!

2. Capitalize the important words in a poetry title.
Directions: With a red crayon, circle the first letter of each word in the title that has more than three letters.

<u>G</u>od is <u>A</u>mazing

3. Put the title in quotations when you refer to the poem in a sentence.
Directions: With a crayon, put a blue square around the quotation marks.

The name of the poem is "God is Amazing"

Take Off

Game

A rhyme is a group of words that have similar endings.

Example

CAT   rhymes with   **HAT**

How To Play:
1. Break group into teams (no more than 2-3 in group)
2. Set timer for 2 minutes.
3. Teacher announces "The rhyming word for today is…" (pause for dramatic effect) and announces the rhyming word for the day.
4. Students write the word on the picture frame.
5. Teacher says, "Go!" Students make a list of as many words that rhyme with the rhyming word of the day.
6. As a group, evaluate the entries. The team that wins receives an extra "Discovery Ticket".

Take Off

Making a Pop-Up Poetry Book

Directions:

1. Make five pop-up pages.
   - Fold construction paper in half widthwise.
   - Make two cuts about one inch apart for each "pop-up".
   - Push folds in opposite direction and crease.
   - Glue onto another piece of folded construction paper for the backing.
2. Decide what part of the design will "pop-up". Draw it and cut it out.
3. Attach drawing to the "pop-up" using tape. Avoid using glue.
4. Design and color a background and foreground.
5. Glue typed poem onto the pop-up page.
6. At the end of the unit, assemble the book by gluing pages together. To help the book lay flat, press with a heavy book overnight.
7. Glue cover with title to the front and Poetry Walk map to the back.
8. When the book is complete, cover with clear contact paper.

The ABC Poem
Creative Worksheet

The "ABC" poem is a fun way to share about your life. It does not have to rhyme.

Example # 1: Each letter stands for an object.

A is for my favorite apple pancakes.
B is for my books that I love to read.
C is for my cat named Shadow who purrs on my lap.
D is for my dad who plays tennis with me.
E is the example that I must set for my siblings.
F is the fun our family has.
G is for God who I love.
H is for the help I need with my math.
I is for an Iguana that I saw at the zoo.
J is for jumping up and down on my bed.
K is for kind words that Mom has said.
L is for love that I am blessed to have.
M is for Mom who makes me sweet bread.
N is for our nanny goat who eats everything.
O is for outside where I love to play.
P is the pool I swim in on hot summer days.
Q is the quiet in my home that only happens at night.
R is for the rabbits we raise.
S is for my doll, Susie.
T is for the tide pools that my family explored.
U is for the unusual family that we are.
V is for the very special times with my friend Tina.
W is for the times we wrestle with my dad.
X is for X-ray they took when I broke my arm.
Y is for my favorite yellow dress.
Z is for the fried zucchini that my mom makes.

The ABC Poem
Creative Worksheet

The "ABC" poem is a fun way to share about your life. It does not have to rhyme.

Example # 2: The letters are used to make sentences.

A girl! That's what I am. Sometimes
Brave and filled with
Courage
Delighted by crafts,
Even sewing.

Few know that I like
Good times playing with my sister on
Hot summer days
In the park,
Jumping like a
Kangaroo.

Loving my
Mom and Dad,
Next, I love my brothers and sisters.

On camping trips and
Playtime, we are not
Quiet but are
Really loud. We
Smile and laugh
Too much sometimes!

Usually I like to dress up in
Very historical costumes and
Wear my hair like
Xerxes living not in Persia but
Yes, living in
Zaire!

© Here To Help Learning • Reproduction prohibited • Flight 2 Launching Paragraph Writing Lesson 17

The ABC Poem
Creative Worksheet

The "ABC" poem is a fun way to share about your life. It does not have to rhyme. You may use example number one or two.

Helpful Hint: If you get stuck on a letter use a picture dictionary or standard dictionary to give you ideas.

A	
B	
C	
D	
E	
F	
G	
H	
I	
J	
K	
L	
M	
N	
O	
P	
Q	
R	
S	
T	
U	
V	
W	
X	
Y	
Z	

Use this map for your poetry book

Directions:
1. Color map.
2. Color the dots next to the poems that you completed in this unit.
3. Connect the dots.
4. Cut out the map and glue it to the back of your poetry book.

Take Off   Game

A rhyme is a group of words that have similar endings.

Example      rhymes with

                  CAT   **HAT**

How To Play:
1. Break group into teams (no more than 2-3 in group)
2. Set timer for 2 minutes.
3. Teacher announces "The rhyming word for today is..." (pause for dramatic effect) and announces the rhyming word for the day.
4. Students write the word on the picture frame.
5. Teacher says, "Go!" Students make a list of as many words that rhyme with the rhyming word of the day.
6. As a group, evaluate the entries. The team that wins receives an extra "Discovery Ticket".

© Here To Help Learning • Reproduction prohibited • Flight 2 Launching Paragraph Writing Lesson 18

Season Poem
Creative Worksheet

God gives us seasons: spring, summer, fall, and winter. They help us tell time and they enable plants to grow. The Seasons poem celebrates the seasons that God gives us.

"...He (God) has shown kindness by giving you rain from heaven and crops in their seasons; He provides you with plenty of food and fills your hearts with joy."
Acts 14:17

The Season poem follows an ABCB rhyming pattern. Let's discover the rhyming pattern. Look at the first verse in the poem below entitled, "Winter".

1. Circle the last word in each line.
2. Label the last word in the first line "A".
3. Label the last word in the second line "A" if it rhymes with the first line or "B" if does NOT rhyme with the last word in the first line.
4. Label the last word in the third line "A" if it rhymes with the first line or "B" if it rhymes with the last word in the second line or "C" if it does NOT rhyme with any of the other words.
5. Look at the last word in the last line. What word does it rhyme with? "A" "B" or "C"

Can you read the rhyming pattern?
Can you discover the rhyming pattern of the second verse?

Student Example **Winter** by Zeke H.	**Which season will you write your poem about?** **Circle one:**
Snowboarding and sled riding _____ Warm jacket and heavy mitten _____ Temperature below zero _____ Cold hands bitten _____ Go inside and get hot chocolate _____ Oh, it makes me warm in my center _____ Toasty on the inside, chilly on the outside _____ This makes winter _____	Spring Summer Fall Winter

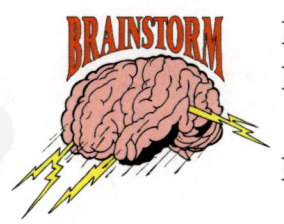

Brainstorm about all the things you love about your chosen season. Follow the instructions for brainstorming in the Language Helps Booklet.

My Season_____

© Here To Help Learning • Reproduction prohibited • Flight 2 Launching Paragraph Writing Lesson 18

Season Poem
Creative Worksheet

The Season poem is written like a recipe. You add items to your poetry mixture to describe the season. It follows an ABCB pattern.

Line one: _____ and _____
                   Add an item   Add an item

Line two: _____ and _____
                   Add an item   Add an item

Line three: _____
                    Add another item and describe it in a creative way.

Line four: _____
                      Add action words (must rhyme with line two).

Line five: _____ and _____
                   Add an item.   Add an item.

Line six: _____ and _____
                  Add an item.   Add an item (must rhyme with line eight).

Line seven: _____
                    Add another item and describe it in a creative way.

Line eight: That makes _____
                              Write your season.

Final Directions: Ask your parent to type your poem and print it for your poetry book. Be sure to use proper grammar. Offer to do something helpful while they type your paper. Be sure to say thank you!

Follow the format below.

Title of your poem
By (Your name)

Your poem

Take Off   Game

A rhyme is a group of words that have similar endings.

Example

CAT   rhymes with   **HAT**

How To Play:
1. Break group into teams (no more than 2-3 in group)
2. Set timer for 2 minutes.
3. Teacher announces "The rhyming word for today is..." (pause for dramatic effect) and announces the rhyming word for the day.
4. Students write the word on the picture frame.
5. Teacher says, "Go!" Students make a list of as many words that rhyme with the rhyming word of the day.
6. As a group, evaluate the entries. The team that wins receives an extra "Discovery Ticket".

© Here To Help Learning • Reproduction prohibited • Flight 2 Launching Paragraph Writing Lesson 19

Nursery Rhyme Poem
Creative Worksheet

Nursery rhymes were written for children in the 1700's. They follow an AABB pattern. They are written to teach a lesson or just to make you smile. Here is one you might know:

Example Poem:

Humpty Dumpty sat on a wall,
Humpty Dumpty had a great fall.
All the king's horses and all the king's men
Couldn't put Humpty together again.

You will have the opportunity to write your own nursery rhyme.
1. Read the student example below.
2. Circle the rhyming pairs and assign a letter starting with the letter A.
3. Continue to discover the rhyming pattern.

Student Example:

Silly Sally Salamander sat on her seat, _____
Pouting and fretting because she couldn't walk down the street. _____
She was so glad that she obeyed and didn't ask why, _____
Because she was rewarded with a juicy fly. _____

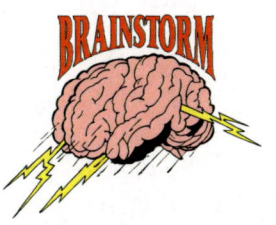

It's time to brainstorm for your Nursery Rhyme poem!
To create a Nursery Rhyme brainstorm for rhyming pairs.
Rhyming pairs:
cat and hat
dig and pig

© Here To Help Learning • Reproduction prohibited • Flight 2 Launching Paragraph Writing Lesson 19

Nursery Rhyme Poem
Creative Worksheet

Line one: _____
                              Rhymes with line 2

Line two: _____
                              Rhymes with line 1

Line three: _____
                              Rhymes with line 4

Line four: _____
                              Rhymes with line 3

Final Directions: Ask your parent to type your poem and print it for your poetry book. Be sure to use proper grammar. Offer to do something helpful while they type your paper. Be sure to say thank you!

Follow the format below.

Title of your poem
By (Your name)

Your poem

Take Off   Game

A rhyme is a group of words that have similar endings.

Example

CAT   rhymes with   **HAT**

How To Play:
1. Break group into teams (no more than 2-3 in group)
2. Set timer for 2 minutes.
3. Teacher announces "The rhyming word for today is..." (pause for dramatic effect) and announces the rhyming word for the day.
4. Students write the word on the picture frame.
5. Teacher says, "Go!" Students make a list of as many words that rhyme with the rhyming word of the day.
6. As a group, evaluate the entries. The team that wins receives an extra "Discovery Ticket".

© Here To Help Learning • Reproduction prohibited • Flight 2 Launching Paragraph Writing Lesson 20

Haiku Poem
Creative Worksheet

A haiku is a Japanese poem that follows a rhythm pattern of 5-7-5.
What does that mean? Each word is made up of syllables or a group of sounds that make a word.

In order to find out how many syllables are in a word, you can try each of the following;

1. You can clap out the syllables.
2. You can also put your hand under your chin as you say each word. Each time your chin hits your hand, you count one syllable.
3. If you are not sure, you may look up the word in a dictionary.

Try clapping or "chin hitting" to hear the different syllables.

Some words only have one syllable: bat, jump, say
Some words have two syllables: for-est, spe-cial, gi-ant
Some words have three syllables: vic-tor-y, yes-ter-day
Some words have four syllables: e-mer-gen-cy, trans-por-ta-tion
Some words have seven syllables: te-le-com-mun-i-ca-tion

Besides having a 5-7-5 pattern, a haiku also has one main idea or subject.

Count the number of syllables in each line.
Write the number of syllables to the left of each line.

Example:

Spring

_____ Spring has come quickly
_____ Butterflies fluttering fast
_____ New growth appears now

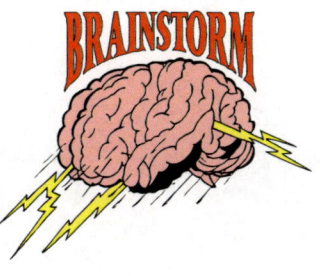

Brainstorm about what subject to use in your haiku. Follow the instructions in the Language Helps Booklet.

After brainstorming, I will write my haiku about

_____

Haiku Poem
Creative Worksheet

Line one: _____
5 syllables

Line two: _____
7 syllables

Line three: _____
5 syllables

Final Directions: Ask your parent to type your poem and print it for your poetry book. Be sure to use proper grammar. Offer to do something helpful while they type your paper. Be sure to say thank you!

Follow the format below.

Title of your poem
By (Your name)

Your poem

Take Off

Game

A rhyme is a group of words that have similar endings.

Example

CAT rhymes with **HAT**

How To Play:
1. Break group into teams (no more than 2-3 in group)
2. Set timer for 2 minutes.
3. Teacher announces "The rhyming word for today is…" (pause for dramatic effect) and announces the rhyming word for the day.
4. Students write the word on the picture frame.
5. Teacher says, "Go!" Students make a list of as many words that rhyme with the rhyming word of the day.
6. As a group, evaluate the entries. The team that wins receives an extra "Discovery Ticket".

Alliteration Poem
Creative Worksheet

Alliteration is the repeating of a certain sound.
Have you ever heard of a tongue twister?
Here is an example of a tongue twister. See if you can say it super fast:

"A little bit of butter makes a bitter batter better."

Now circle the all the letter "B's" in the tongue twister.

How many words start with the letter "B"?_____

The repetition of the "B" sound is called alliteration.

Another Example:

Why do dancing ducks dash downtown?
To dine and drink double thick desserts.

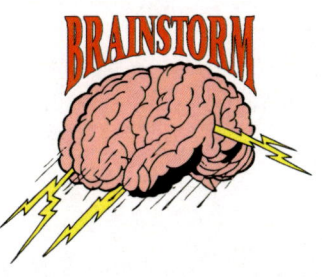

Brainstorm: What subject will you use for your Alliteration poem. Follow the instructions in the Language Helps Booklet.

After brainstorming, I will write my poem

about_____ and I will use the letter _____

Alliteration Poem
Creative Worksheet

Helpful hint: Use a dictionary to find words that start with the same letter.

Line 1:

_____

_____

Ask a question

Line 2:

_____

_____

Answer the question

Final Directions: Ask your parent to type your poem and print it for your poetry book. Be sure to use proper grammar. Offer to do something helpful while they type your paper. Be sure to say thank you!

Follow the format below.

Title of your poem
By (Your name)

Your poem

Dear President
Writing Project 5

The Writing Process — Dear President

Brainstorm	
Make a List	
Webbing	
First Rough Draft	
First Input (Content Focus)	
Second Rough Draft	
Second Input (Grammar & Spelling Focus)	
Final Recopy	
Publish	

Take Off — Game

Transitional words help connect your ideas together.
Transitional words help your writing to read more smoothly.

HOW TO PLAY:

1. Turn to the Transitional and Linking Words section of the Language Helps Booklet.
2. Choose a column of transitional words. Example: Add Information
3. Using the first word in the column, the teacher begins to tell a story.
4. Students take turns continuing the story using the words on the list until the last word is used.

Remember: It is okay to be silly, just make sure you are God honoring!

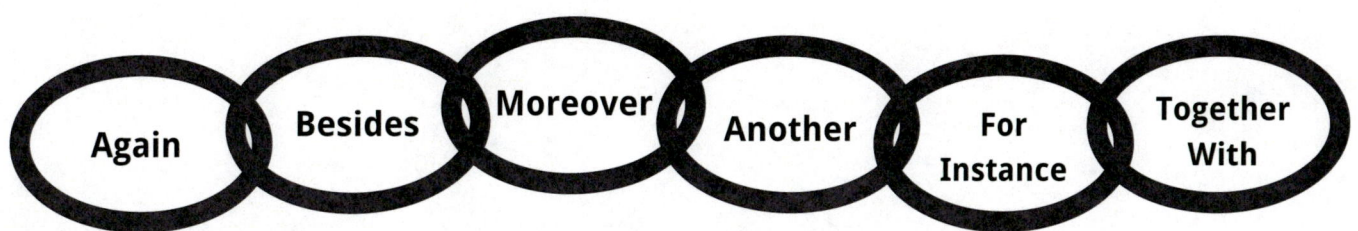

© Here To Help Learning • Reproduction prohibited • Flight 2 Launching Paragraph Writing Lesson 22

Dear President

Do you think it would be hard to be president? I think it would! That is why we are called by God to pray for our leaders.

> *"I urge, then, first of all, that petitions, prayers, intercession and thanksgiving be made for all people—for kings and all those in authority, that we may live peaceful and quiet lives in all godliness and holiness."* **1 Timothy 2:1-2**

We are blessed in America to have the opportunity to give input to our leaders. However, when we share our input, we are also instructed to do it respectfully.

> *"Show proper respect to everyone, love the family of believers, fear God, honor the emperor (government leader)."* **1 Peter 2:17**

In this project, we will use PIP (Praise, Input, Praise) and respectful words to share our ideas with our president. We will also learn about a special letter-writing format called a Business Letter Format. This format also shows respect.

Another part about sharing input with someone is taking the time to understand another person's position and seeing life from their point of view. Jesus called this compassion. Compassion can be described as getting into another person's shoes and imagining what life is like for them.

Discuss: What do you think life is like for the President of the United States?

The tone of our voice changes when we have compassion. Tone is a literary technique or a special way a writer writes to help their readers feel the story. To understand tone, let's read out loud three sentences that are exactly the same. As we read them, we will only change the way we say it or the tone of how we say it.

(Happy)- Please, go into the car.
(Tired)- Please, go into the car.
(Angry)- Please, go into the car.
(Respectful)- Please, go into the car.

 **Talk about it:** How did the meaning of the sentences change as we changed the tone of our voice?

God gives us instructions on how we should say our words.

> *"A gentle answer turns away wrath, but a harsh word stirs up anger."*
> **Proverbs 15:1**

In this project, we will learn to write with a respectful tone as we share our praise and input with the president.

© Here To Help Learning • Reproduction prohibited • Flight 2 Launching Paragraph Writing Lesson 22

Full Throttle

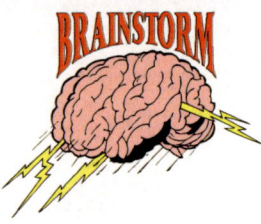

Let's brainstorm together! We will do two brainstorming sessions today. First, brainstorm about the things you like about America and then brainstorm about the things you would like to change in America to make it a better place for all of us to live.

Directions: Follow the brainstorming technique found in the Language Helps Booklet.

Make A List

Project Name: Dear President

Directions: Complete the chart below.

PRAISE
These are the things that I could say thank you to the president for:

1. _____

2. _____

3. _____

4. _____

INPUT
These are things that I would like to change in America and how I would change them.

I would like to see these things changed in America	How will the changes help America?

PRAISE
These are the things that I think are wonderful about America:

1. _____

2. _____

3. _____

4. _____

© Here To Help Learning • Reproduction prohibited • Flight 2 Launching Paragraph Writing Lesson 22

Take Off

Writing Warm-up

Name _____

Word Box

Look at the picture. Choose 6 words that describe the picture. Write the words in the boxes. Use them in a sentence or create a story.

© Here To Help Learning • Reproduction prohibited • Flight 2 Launching Paragraph Writing Lesson 23

Full Throttle

Webbing

Project name: Dear President

Directions: Look at your list from last lesson and group like ideas into the three unshaded ovals. In the top shaded oval, write a fabulous attention-getter sentence. In the last shaded oval, add a wonderful closing sentence. Remember, you do not have to use all of your list items.

Attention-Getter Sentence
Thank the president.

Praise- What do you like about America?

Input- What changes would you like to see and how will the changes help America?

Praise- Thank the president again!

Closing Sentence
Encourage the president.

© Here To Help Learning • Reproduction prohibited • Flight 2 Launching Paragraph Writing Lesson 23

Take Off

Writing Warm-up

Name_____

Word Box

Look at the picture. Choose 6 words that describe the picture. Write the words in the boxes. Use them in a sentence or create a story.

© Here To Help Learning • Reproduction prohibited • Flight 2 Launching Paragraph Writing Lesson 24

Full Throttle

How to Write a Business Letter

Directions: Follow the format below:

Date
> Date

Sender's Address
> Your Full Name
> Your Address
> Your City, State and Zip Code

President's Address
> President _____
> The White House
> 1600 Pennsylvania Avenue NW
> Washington, DC 20500

Salutation
> Dear (President's Name) :

Body
> The body of the letter includes the information that you would like to share with the president.

Print
> Thank you,
> Your Printed Name

Signature
> Your Signature

Full Throttle

I Can Help! First Input

Project name: Dear President

Name of Student Presenting: _____

Input Questions	Yes	No	More Please!	Not Needed
Is there an attention-getting sentence?				
Is there a closing sentence?				
Do the sentences flow together?				
Is there enough content?				
Are there transitional words?				
Does the author stay on task with the project instructions?				
🎨 Are there words that help the reader see?				
🎨 Are there words that help the reader hear?				
🎨 Are there words that help the reader feel?				
🎨 Are there words that help the reader smell?				
🎨 Are there words that help the reader taste?				

Praise-

Input-

Praise-

Change these DEAD WORDS:

_____

_____

_____

For instructions on how to change a dead word, see the Language Helps Booklet.

© Here To Help Learning • Permission to copy page • Flight 2 Launching Paragraph Writing Lesson 25

Making an Essay Folder

Step 1. *Create your Essay Folder.*

1. Gather Supplies
   - 12"X18" construction paper- any color
   - Long arm stapler
   - 5-6 copies of lined paper.

2. Fold construction paper in half widthwise.

3. Place 5-6 copies of lined paper on the lower half of the folded construction paper. Using a long arm stapler, staple the top of the lined paper to the construction paper.

4. Fold the construction paper back over the lined paper. Using a glue stick, attach the cover to the front of the essay folder.

Step 2. *Use the lesson cover template on the next page.*

Ideas:
Decorate the cover with pictures from your story.
Use borders and color in the background.
Be creative!

Sample Essay Folder Cover For This Project

© Here To Help Learning • Reproduction prohibited • Flight 2 Launching Paragraph Writing Lesson 26

Story Box Fiction
Writing Project 6

The Writing Process — Story Box Fiction

Brainstorm	
Make a List	
Webbing	
First Rough Draft	
First Input (Content Focus)	
Second Rough Draft	
Second Input (Grammar & Spelling Focus)	
Final Recopy	
Publish	

Take Off

Writing Warm-up

Name_____

Word Box

Look at the picture. Choose 6 words that describe the picture. Write the words in the boxes. Use them in a sentence or create a story.

© Here To Help Learning • Reproduction prohibited • Flight 2 Launching Paragraph Writing Lesson 27

What is Fiction?

Fiction is a story that is not true. There are different types of fiction. There is **historical fiction**, where some of the events are true, but the characters are not true. An example of historical fiction would be a story about a mouse in the Revolutionary War times. There is **science fiction**, where the science portion of the story may be partly true, but most of it is the imagination of the author. An example of science fiction would be a shrinking machine that enables people to "walk" through the human body. **Fanciful fiction** takes place in imaginary lands with fairytale characters. For your project, you may choose any type of fiction.

Circle the type of fiction that you want to write:

Historical fiction

Science fiction

Fanciful fiction

Story Box Fiction Project: Setting is important in a fictional story. It helps your reader to feel like they are a part of the story. Throughout this unit, you will make a story box that will show the setting of your fictional story. Use your story box for writing ideas.

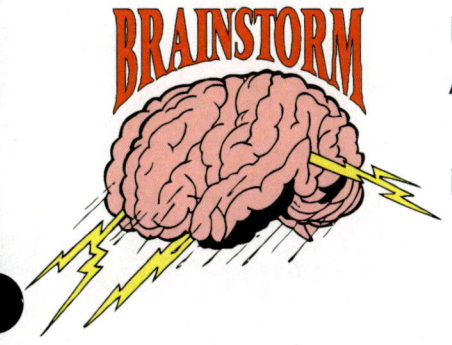

Project name: Story Box Fiction
After brainstorming together, my story will take place

in _____.

Full Throttle

Make A List

Project name: Story Box Fiction

Directions:
Make a list of each part of your story by drawing pictures and adding descriptive words. You may use more notebook paper if needed.

The characters- Draw the characters in your story. Add descriptive words around your picture.

The Setting- Draw the setting in your story. Add descriptive words around your picture.

© Here To Help Learning • Reproduction prohibited • Flight 2 Launching Paragraph Writing Lesson 27

Make A List

The Conflict- Draw the conflict in your story. Add descriptive words around your picture.

The Conflict-Solved- Draw how the conflict in your story will be solved. Add descriptive words around your picture.

Main Idea or the lesson learned _____

_____

© Here To Help Learning • Reproduction prohibited • Flight 2 Launching Paragraph Writing Lesson 27

How to Make a Story Box
In lesson 28-32, you will create a story box.

1. Get a shoebox.

2. Cover the outside the box with construction paper.

3. Create a background with construction paper.

4. Create a setting.

5. Add your characters.

6. Add details.

Helpful Hint: To make items in your box stand up, make a cardboard triangle and attach your item.

© Here To Help Learning • Reproduction prohibited • Flight 2 Launching Paragraph Writing Lesson 27

Student Writing Evaluation

Name _____ Writing Project: <u>Dear President</u>

My best sentence was _____

_____

_____

I like this sentence because _____

_____

_____

I could improve my writing on my next project by _____

_____

_____

_____ Yes, I published my project

Parent Note:

Co-Op Teachers Note:

© Here To Help Learning • Reproduction prohibited • Flight 2 Launching Paragraph Writing Lesson 27

Take Off
Game

Directions: Complete the sentences below using a single word or groups of words.
Important Vocabulary:
Noun- A person, place, or thing
Adjective- A word that describes noun
Challenge: Make up your own similes and metaphors!

 # Similes Make Me Smile!

A simile is a comparison that uses the words like or as.
Write a simile by completing the sentences below.
You can be silly, just remember to be God-honoring.

The star is _____ as a_____.
               (adjective)   *(noun)*

The star was _____ like a_____.
                (adjective)   *(noun)*

 # I'm All for Metaphors

A metaphor is a comparison that DOES NOT use the words like or as.
Write a metaphor by completing the sentence below.
You can be silly, just remember to be God-honoring.

The star has the sparkle of _____.
                                        (Choose a noun that describes the star's sparkle.)

How to Activate the Gigglebox:

 You can find the Gigglebox 3000 at heretohelplearning.com/gigglebox or scan the QR Code to the left with your smartphone.

© Here To Help Learning • Reproduction prohibited • Flight 2 Launching Paragraph Writing Lesson 28

Take Off

Writing Warm-up

Name_____

Word Box

Look at the picture. Choose 6 words that describe the picture. Write the words in the boxes. Use them in a sentence or create a story.

© Here To Help Learning • Reproduction prohibited • Flight 2 Launching Paragraph Writing Lesson 28

Full Throttle

Webbing

Project name: Story Box Fiction

Directions: Look at your list from last week. Group like ideas into the three shaded ovals. In the top shaded oval, write a fabulous attention-getter sentence and in the last shaded oval, add a wonderful closing sentence.

Attention-Getter Sentence

Beginning- Setting

Middle- Conflict

End- Conflict Resolved

Closing Sentence
Theme or main idea

© Here To Help Learning • Reproduction prohibited • Flight 2 Launching Paragraph Writing Lesson 28

Take Off
Game

Directions: Complete the sentences below using a single word or groups of words.
Important Vocabulary:
Noun- A person, place, or thing
Adjective- A word that describes noun
Challenge: Make up your own similes and metaphors!

 # Similes Make Me Smile!

A simile is a comparison that uses the words like or as.
Write a simile by completing the sentences below.
You can be silly, just remember to be God-honoring.

The car is _____ as a _____.
　　　　　　　(adjective)　　　　　　　　　　　　　(noun)

The car was _____ like a _____.
　　　　　　　(adjective)　　　　　　　　　　　　　(noun)

 # I'm All for Metaphors

A metaphor is a comparison that DOES NOT use the words like or as.
Write a metaphor by completing the sentence below.
You can be silly, just remember to be God-honoring.

The car's engine had the sound of a _____.
　　　　　　　　　　　　　　　　　　　　(Choose a noun that describes the car's engine.)

How to Activate the Gigglebox:

You can find the Gigglebox 3000 at
heretohelplearning.com/gigglebox
or scan the QR Code to the left
with your smartphone.

© Here To Help Learning • Reproduction prohibited • Flight 2 Launching Paragraph Writing Lesson 29

Take Off

Writing Warm-up

Name_____

Word Box

Look at the picture. Choose 6 words that describe the picture. Write the words in the boxes. Use them in a sentence or create a story.

© Here To Help Learning • Reproduction prohibited • Flight 2 Launching Paragraph Writing Lesson 29

Full Throttle

I Can Help! First Input

Project name: Story Box Fiction

Name of Student Presenting: _____

Input Questions	Yes	No	More Please!	Not Needed
Is there an attention-getting sentence?				
Is there a closing sentence?				
Do the sentences flow together?				
Is there enough content?				
Are there transitional words?				
Does the author stay on task with the project instructions?				
🎨 Are there words that help the reader see?				
🎨 Are there words that help the reader hear?				
🎨 Are there words that help the reader feel?				
🎨 Are there words that help the reader smell?				
🎨 Are there words that help the reader taste?				

Praise-

Input-

Praise-

Change these DEAD WORDS:

_____
_____
_____

For instructions on how to change a dead word, see the Language Helps Booklet.

© Here To Help Learning • Permission to copy page • Flight 2 Launching Paragraph Writing Lesson 30

Making an Essay Folder

Step 1. Create your Essay Folder.

1. Gather Supplies
   - 12"X18" construction paper- any color
   - Long arm stapler
   - 5-6 copies of lined paper.

2. Fold construction paper in half widthwise.

3. Place 5-6 copies of lined paper on the lower half of the folded construction paper. Using a long arm stapler, staple the top of the lined paper to the construction paper.

4. Fold the construction paper back over the lined paper. Using a glue stick, attach the cover to the front of the essay folder.

Step 2. Use the lesson cover template on the next page.

Ideas:
Decorate the cover with pictures from your story.
Use borders and color in the background.
Be creative!

Sample Essay Folder Cover For This Project

Student Writing Evaluation

Name _____   Writing Project: <u>Story Box Fiction</u>

My best sentence was _____

_____

_____

I like this sentence because _____

_____

_____

I could improve my writing on my next project by _____

_____

_____

_____ Yes, I published my project

Parent Note:

Co-Op Teachers Note: